"I think there is a dire need for fresh expecta ship and a dire need for leaders to get out of the box more often. Too much of today's thinking about almost everything is yesterday's. This stimulating book makes you think new about what leadership should be now and should help each of us raise our levels of success and to believe that we are making things better."

MARY WELLS LAWRENCE

First woman CEO of a company listed on the New York Stock Exchange, American Advertising Federation Hall of Famer

"This book offers a creative lens for examining how to become a more responsive, innovative, and effective leader. It provides a unique and compelling perspective for improving your organizational efforts."

DON FINLESS

President, The Onix Group of Companies, Ottawa, Canada. Design, animation, and IT solutions

"This book is a valuable resource for anybody who leads an enterprise in an increasingly complex, dynamic and global world. The AGILE approach delivers leadership and strategy that is effective and appropriate."

ERIC BOHM

CEO, World Wildlife Fund (WWF), Hong Kong

"*The Agile Business Leader* cuts straight to the core of today's challenge for business leaders driving a high velocity, global, and cross-generational workforce."

PAUL RINGMACHER

Partner, Financial Services Technology, Capco

"In a current environment that often provides a dark back-drop for business, Barry and Eileen deliver a very timely message that precisely cracks the code for contemporary organizational success. *The Agile Business Leader* provides a formula of necessary leadership traits that will define success in the coming decade."

R. KARL SCHLATZER

Director, Global Business Development and Channels, SAS

"Historically, business leadership was autocratic and definitely 'top down'. What this book explores with fresh insight is how modern managers and leaders work with their teams to achieve results. AGILE leaders encourage original thought at all levels of the organisation and empower a far greater number of people."

KEITH BUTLER-WHEELHOUSE

CEO Smith's Group in London. Also served as CEO of Saab Automobiles in Sweden, chairman and CEO of Delta Motor Corporation, and director, General Motors South Africa

THE AGILE BUSINESS LEADER SERIES

❖ The Agile Business Leader ⊗

The Four Roles of Successful Leaders

No one leadership style is universally satisfactory. The leader who can listen, delegate, involve, decide, adapt, respond, and direct is the most successful over time. In an era filled with confusion, contradictions, and corruption, the world is calling for Agile Business Leaders.

❖ The Strategist ❖

ABL Theory in Practice

Strategists are always asking, "What's next?" "Where else?" and "Why not?" They have an inquisitive nature, helping to create a sense of identity for people in their organization. Seeking large gains and unafraid to take smart, calculated risks, Strategists work on one simple rule: explore outside the boundaries with quantum-leap thinking.

❖ The Specialist ❖

ABL Theory in Practice

Specialists recognize that having a diverse knowledge and experience base enables them to assimilate novel ideas and connect seemingly discrete pieces of information. Specialists can quickly analyze a situation, make decisions, and act on opportunities.

❖ The Champion ❖

ABL Theory in Practice

Champions are responsive and authentic, regularly surpassing their personal goals by having the courage to do what is right. They grow excited about the possibilities that new ideas can bring. Champions personify corporate values and help form the character and strength of the organization.

❖ The Enabler ❖

ABL Theory in Practice

Enablers are not about authority; they are about influence, loyalty, and trust. They have strong collaboration skills and continually seek out ways to engage the masses and build organizations that continually learn, adapt, evolve, and improve.

THE AGILE BUSINESS LEADER®

THE ROLE OF THE CHAMPION

THE AGILE BUSINESS LEADER®

Eileen Dowse ❖ Barry Brewster

BROWSE PUBLISHING LIMITED

London • Hong Kong • Sydney • Dallas

Email: info@agilebusinessleader.com

Website: www.agilebusinessleader.com

ISBN: 978-988-19468-5-0

Cover Design: Bonnie Brewster

Text Design and epub composition: Jean Boles

Graphic Design: Bonnie Brewster

Text Artwork: Tim Hamons

Cartaphors: GroupM, Firsttrack, Aedas

Copyeditor: Jean Boles

CONTENTS

x

ACKNOWLEDGMENTS

This book evolved over four years of working with thousands of people in their roles as leaders, employees, and learners. It is intended as a tribute to these people who shared their learning and frustrations with us over the years. *The Agile Business Leader* reflects the efforts and influences of many people. Certain people gave themselves to this work in large ways that call for special thanks.

We want to express our deepest appreciation to the unique leaders who were interviewed for this book, including Scott Andrews, Finn Boyer, Dan Duran, Patrick Carmichael, E'Vonne Cole, Jeff Daniels, Bobby Feilger, Leona Freed, Jeremy Gwee, Ian Hanna, Kay Holt, Howard Holtman, Mark Moran, Mark Patterson, David Roberts, David Spann, Karl Schlatzer, and Genelle Sharples. It has been a privilege to work with these individuals and gain clarity on their insights so we can share them with readers.

We also wish to thank the organizations, authors, and leaders who granted us permission to use figures, information, and quotes. We especially wish to acknowledge the leaders and staff at Evans & Peck for allowing us to use their case studies. It was here that our ideas were helped to incubate. We particularly thank GroupM, the Venetian Casino, Firsttrack, and Aedas, which agreed to share their Cartaphors with us and let others learn from their experiences.

We both want to especially thank our proofreaders Maria L. den Boer, and Lyn Brewster. Their reviews provided thoughtful guidance and constructive feedback.

We are extremely grateful to our graphic designer Bonnie Brewster, who produced the book design concept and the many diagrams throughout the books. Tim Hamons, you have been wonderful in producing almost 200 sketches, which allowed us to share our message with clarity and character.

Jean Boles has joined our team after the initial ABL book was published and has taken over the editing role seamlessly; a very big thank you.

In addition, Eileen also thanks her wise friend Claudia Dubois, who helped to provide support and encouragement for completing this book. Eileen thanks her longtime friend Lauri Andrews, whose good humor and generous spirit endured many supportive phone calls and long talks as this book evolved. Finally Eileen knows that she could not have written this book without the faith and support of her husband of thirty-five years, David Dowse, and their children, Bryan, Kathleen and John.

Barry wishes to thank his "commercial mentor," friend and colleague Colin Jesse, who has guided his development in corporate governance and commercial reality over the past twelve years. Without his support and guidance Barry would not have been a position to be able to write this book. Chris Brooks also provided patient and insightful support in helping to validate the concepts and models throughout the book.

Barry also thanks his inspirational and loving wife Lyn and children, Martin, Bonnie and her husband Luke Edwards plus mother Dorothy Barnes, who at 80-plus years is still an inspiration. As Tom Cruise said once, "You complete me!"

Note: We have made every effort to acknowledge the original creators of concepts presented in this book. If we have not succeeded in that endeavor we are sorry and would like to hear from you so that we can begin referencing your work.

THE CHAMPION

❖ *Demonstrates Capabilities* ❖

If you don't stand for something you might fall for anything.

ALICE COOPER
Lyric from his song, "Stand"

INTRODUCTION

PURPOSE OF THIS BOOK

The purpose of this book, pure and simple, examines each of the Champion's traits and competencies more closely and includes additional theory to our introduction book, *The Agile Business Leader*, to provide you opportunities and tools for practicing each ABL role. It is designed to enable you to do your job better, faster, more accurately, and more efficiently and to be more economical—with less stress! *The Agile Business Leader* is designed to provide a common language for leaders at all levels. Our goal is to provide business leaders with a primer on practices and tools for functioning in a world of complexity, chaos, interdependency, and ambiguity. Developing leadership capabilities often requires changing people's mindset and altering their long-standing beliefs. It entails recognizing the causes and effects of peak learning and developing strategies for mental blocks, blind spots, and other barriers. This book offers readers some ideas that will withstand the test of time. An ABL thrives on communication and sharing of ideas and practices. This book is relevant to anyone who wants to begin understanding different insights and approaches for dealing with the human capital within her or his organization or team and accelerating results. It will identify aspects of building effective relationships, dialogue, and commitment. We know that good leaders develop through a never-ending process of self-study, education, training, and experience. This book requires that you be willing to learn strategies, recognize your own leadership style, and transfer knowledge to the workplace for improving collaboration, communication, and productivity. Regardless of whether you are a new or experienced leader, this book will help you to develop and strengthen your skills and enable you to take responsibility for your development. Although the concepts presented in this book were developed specifically for leaders, they are useful concepts for all individuals in all kinds of professions.

Information presented in this book can be used for

- Starting new initiatives.
- Maximizing the effectiveness of communications.
- Gaining a competitive edge.
- Exemplifying corporate governance.
- Mobilizing and incorporating existing talents.
- Creating paths to more profitability.
- Building collaborative cultures.

OVERVIEW OF STRUCTURE

In this book you will be introduced to concepts and tools designed to enable you to implement them into your own work. We have structured this book around the ABL model. Book 1 explains the elements of the model and the principles of being an Agile Business Leader. This book elaborates on one of the four roles that constitute Agile Business Leadership, and this book will provide theory and practice opportunities to develop a broader understanding of the practical and theoretical aspects of leadership and give you the opportunity to learn more about a variety of perspectives on how to become more agile in your approach. If you are leader with an interest in performance and productivity, we believe you will find great value in this book.

MESSAGE TO OUR READERS

We hope this book provides you with useful ideas and insights. We look forward to hearing about your models, approaches, and experiences as you read through this material. We are sure we have only begun to scratch the surface of developing Agile Business Leaders.

Please email us at mail@agilebusinessleader.com with your comments and ideas, or visit our website at

www.agilebusinessleader.com.

1

THE AGILE
BUSINESS LEADER

ABL MODEL

As mentioned in our first book, *The Agile Business Leader, The Four Roles of Successful Leaders,* Agile Business Leadership is more than a mindset; it is a set of roles, traits, and competencies focused on organizational and individual components. These traits are crucial for every leader in every culture and in every industry. When we talked to Australian leaders working in the Philippines, they said, "It's challenging to work in this country because of all the corruption involved and the requirement for doing business." When we talked to U.S. leaders working in a controversial startup, they said, "Traditional organizations are a bunch of babies and need to realize that things are going to change and we plan to make sure of that." When we talked to leaders in the Middle East, they said, "As with all things in the Middle East, relationship building is 80 percent of the game and things just slow down due to various factors—bureaucracy, ego, heat, and communication." When we talked with leaders in Costa Rica, they said, "We were having so much trouble getting work done and communicating what we wanted. Then we learned that the word "dialogue: in Spanish means "to argue." and began to realize why none of the workers wanted to "dialogue: with us to resolve the issues." When we talked with leaders in Denmark about working with people in the United States, they said, "Why are people being so polite in this meeting? Get to the point, be direct, and stop apologizing and saying thank you all the time." When we talked with telecommunication leaders in Paris, France, they told us they must strategize differently because "the market force is evaporating and changing because there are less and less customers due to large communication companies buying smaller ones and putting them out of business and this makes the market smaller."

It's easy to understand why it is a challenge for successful leaders to work in a global economy. Not only must they "follow the sun" while doing business, they must meet the requirements of their industry and culture. There is an enormous amount of factors to take into consideration when leading with an organization. The ABL model is a performance model providing the bedrock of required skills and abilities for any leader who wants to positively impact success. This model has its underpinnings in the idea of social and emotional intelligence, since it involves an ability to manage oneself in the context of interpersonal relations. In other words, to be an effective leader one must be able to perform a task with an appropriate level of interpersonal skills, professional knowledge, and operational ability to achieve the goal. These ABL components can be driven from both internal and external sources. The model emphasizes self-awareness, engagement techniques, know-ledge, and methods for business development. The ABL model is deceptively simple. It answers the question, "What type of leadership is needed in the current world of business?"

When developing this model we drew from our work with clients from around the world. A theory emerged as we helped to provide clients with a meaningful description for which types of elements are needed by a leader in today's emerging markets. This model offers concepts that have stood the test of time and that we believe are equally relevant for the tough challenges that lie ahead.

Agile Business Leaders consistently and successfully face two realities:

i) The need to be business-AND people-focused, and
ii) The expectation that they build personal and organizational competencies AND achieve action.

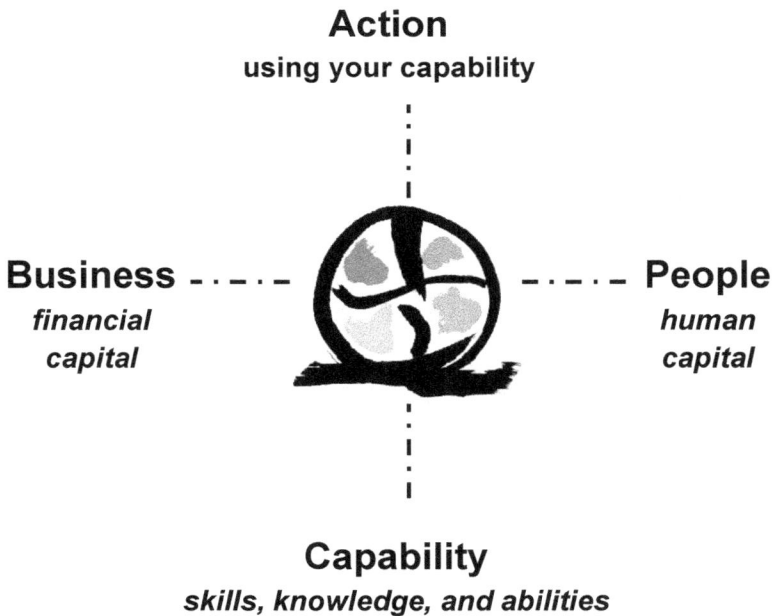

Action
using your capability

Business - - - - -   - - - - - **People**
financial   *human*
capital   *capital*

Capability
skills, knowledge, and abilities

THE HORIZONTAL REALITY

A reality for leaders is working with i) Business (financial capital—wealth employed for the production of more wealth) and ii) People (human capital—the sum total of an organization's human performance capability). The horizontal line of this model addresses the factors impacting the success of an organization.

```
┌─────────────┐                          ┌─────────────┐
│  Business   │                          │   People    │
│  financial  │ _ . _ . _ . Agility _ . _ . _ . _ │   human     │
│   capital   │                          │   capital   │
└─────────────┘                          └─────────────┘
```

Business includes assets, liabilities, and equity. It includes the money, securities, property, and other valuables that collectively represent the wealth of the business and are used to generate income by investing in either a business or different income sources. Business capital is the net worth of a business, or in simpler terms, the amount by which the organization's assets exceed its liabilities. The Business side of this model also includes the mission, goals, values, and vision for the organization. It includes the methods and practices an organization endorses to achieve financial well-being.

People includes the collective human resources of the organization that contribute to organizational performance. An organization's human capital is the collective sum of the attributes, life experience, knowledge, inventiveness, energy, and enthusiasm that its people choose to invest in their work. It incorporates the group dynamics, values, norms, attitudes, motivational forces, and collaboration. It is the organization's human ecosystem, or more simply put, the personality of the organization. The People side is the accumulated present value of the employees. It is the component of the organization that drives the organization and influences strategic operations, employee loyalty, and commitment.

THE VERTICAL REALITY

Another reality of Capabilities (an individual's unique knowledge, skills, and abilities) and Action (turning talent into effective responses) addresses the components of character and behavior.

Action
using your capability

ı
.
ı

Agility

.
ı
.
ı

Capability
skills, knowledge, and abilities

Action includes the ability to transform knowledge and talent into actions. Action involves sensing changes in signals from the environment (both internal and external) and the ability to adapt accordingly. In addition, it includes developing and communicating strategic initiatives, adapting current operations to improve effectiveness, implementing new business directions, motivating people to achieve results, and aligning oneself around the direction of the organization. The Action side of this model also includes the methods and practices an organization needs to create, capture, transfer, and mobilize knowledge to enable the organization to adapt to a changing environment.

Capability includes the sum of the individual's knowledge, skills, and attributes. Capability focuses on the uniqueness of the individual and his or her expertise, natural aptitude, acquired proficiency, and capacity to perform. Capability refers to both a person's ability to learn in the future and actions that he or she can do now. It incorporates consistent behavior and a degree of mental capacity and moral quality. These two realities—Business & People and Action & Capability—can be used to form a model for understanding the roles, traits, and competencies needed to be an Agile Business Leader.

When the two realities are crossed, four quadrants are created to define the four roles of an Agile Business Leader: (1) Strategist, (2) Enabler, (3) Champion, and (4) Specialist. Each of these roles comes with a list of traits and competencies associated with them. Our thinking is that a leader must have ALL traits in order to be effective.

2

THE ABL CHAMPION

It takes all the running you can do, to keep in the same place.

LEWIS CARROLL

The Champion responds to the realities of needing to be peo-ple-focused while needing to have the capabilities to perform. Champions are focused on helping the group dynamics of the or-ganization by positively focusing on current and past strengths, successes, and potentials while mobilizing and incorporating his own talents to achieve the end results.

The four traits of the Champion are:

- Resourceful
- Responsive
- Resilient
- Committed

Champions recognize that speed and responsiveness have become more important than ever for business survival. Getting people excited about people performing quality work, staying committed to the cause, and moving forward toward profitability are major components for overall success. Champions are responsive, authentic, and willing to expose themselves by having the courage to do what is right. They get excited about the possibilities that new ideas can bring. Champions personify corporate values and help form the character and the strength of the organization. They have the courage to stand up for what they believe and have a strong orientation toward achievement. They have high expectations for themselves and for others and always push to achieve. In short, the Champion's role is related to the leader's character.

Personifying a Champion is all but forgotten by modern standards. Traditionally, corporations value leaders who are rational and are strategic thinkers who develop excellent systems. This old way of thinking valued people who *ran* the organization. Today, organizations need Champions who continually *create* the organization as it responds to ever-changing business demands. Creating an organization and leading people successfully is achieved by a leader with a strong character, confidence, and courage.

The Need for Champions

We know through our work that people have become the driving force of business success. When we talk to our clients and other global leaders about what makes an organization successful, from the perspective of its people and their capabilities, the overwhelming response we hear is that "leadership quality impacts success." Leaders create value for stakeholders and respond quickly to customers' needs.

Leaders who are trustworthy and courageous enough to make the "tough calls" are the ones who earn the respect of people following them.

We have heard it said that if you want to find out how good tea can be, put it in hot water. The same is true for Champions. You can tell how good Champions are by the way they deal with crises, ethical issues, attacks on their character, and by their need to stand up for what they believe is right.

Champions have existed throughout history. You might have heard stories about great leaders who fostered innovation, built commitment, engaged the masses, and aligned people to a vision. In the book, *The King Alfred Millenary: A Record of the Proceedings of the National Commemoration*, British novelist, Sir Walter Besant, talks about King Alfred as being a model for great leadership. Besant states, "There is none like Alfred in the whole page of history, none with a record altogether so blameless, none so wise, none so human. He is truly a leader."

This excerpt catches our attention. What made King Alfred a great leader? Known for his wisdom, competence, and moral nobility, upon further investigation we learn that he became famous for his courage and skill as a warrior. King Alfred valiantly defended England against a stronger enemy, the Vikings and the Danes. He understood the value of diplomacy and formed amicable relations for securing peace. Alfred was also devoted to the welfare of his people. He rebuilt structures, imported foreign scholars, founded schools, and personally learned Latin in order to translate books into English so his people could improve their literacy. He assisted people in learning.

We agree that accomplishing these feats makes a leader great. We also know that a lot of these characteristics are incorporated today in capabilities of the Champion. Champions present themselves to the world as confident, adaptable, responsive, and perseverant people. They have an intense work ethic, are disciplined, and are unruffled by provocations. They are dynamic ambassadors who consistently maintain integrity, overcome resistance, and promote a unity of purpose. They assume strategic responsibilities, and their contribution to the growth of the business can be easily identified. They understand that they have value. The Champion has the wisdom and innovation to work cross-functionally by influencing, inspiring, and leveraging optimization and utilizing the strengths of the organization. Champions have the courage to try new approaches and do what no one else does. They are worth watching and emulating.

Champions are ordinary heroes who do extraordinary acts under the right circumstances. They know what is expected of them and have the confidence to be innovative in whatever way they can to get the job done. They have both the skill and the will to do the right thing, at the right time, in the right way, and for the right reason. In a way, the Champion's role could be considered a global currency for business, because the capabilities possessed in this area are valued around the world.

The case for becoming a Champion is compelling since speed in anticipating and responding to customer demands and quality in delivering results continue to be important ingredients of competitive advantage. Champions have the passion to strive and surpass their personal goals because they are relentless and consistent.

Champion Traits and Competencies
The ABL Champion integrates four traits with seven competencies to leverage a unique market position and sustain future growth.

The four Champion traits along with the accompanying competencies are as follows:

Resourceful:

1. Use innovative practices to influence and adjust.
2. Build internal and external networks.

Responsive:

3. Understand self and use strengths.
4. Set high expectations.

Resilient:

5. Practice work/life balance.

Committed:

6. Act with courage.
7. Achieve with self-determination.

The following sections of this book describe how each of these competencies supports the four traits that define the Champion's role.

3

CHAMPION TRAIT #1

▲ Resourceful ▼

"Supreme resourcefulness consists in knowing the value of things."

FRANÇOIS DE LA ROCHEFOUCAULD
French writer

Being resourceful is different from using your resources. Being resourceful centers on being able to make the most of a situation with the immediate amenities you have at hand. Resourcefulness incorporates perspective, innovation, and the ability to create solutions in a way that may be different from the usual.

Most people don't see the world as it is; they see it as they are. The resourceful champion sees the bigger picture. Being resourceful involves

- Suspending judgment and having healthy skepticism.

- Thinking of outrageous (and practical) possibilities for designing workable solutions (in some cases for their own survival).

- Experimenting with different perspectives when assessing situations and resolving issues.

- Going against conventional wisdom and societal norms when addressing challenges.

- Taking stock of what is available and applying it toward the solution

THEORY IN PRACTICE ACTIVITY 3.1

MAXIMIZE YOUR RESOURCES

Objective of this exercise: To help you assess your creative use of resources by understanding how you perceive givens, restraints, and opportunities.

Instructions:

Step 1: *Drawing.* In five minutes, sketch objects or pictures that have circles as a major part of the image on the diagram on the following page.

$$\bigcirc \quad \bigcirc \quad \bigcirc \quad \bigcirc$$

$$\bigcirc \quad \bigcirc \quad \bigcirc \quad \bigcirc$$

$$\bigcirc \quad \bigcirc \quad \bigcirc \quad \bigcirc$$

$$\bigcirc \quad \bigcirc \quad \bigcirc \quad \bigcirc$$

$$\bigcirc \quad \bigcirc \quad \bigcirc \quad \bigcirc$$

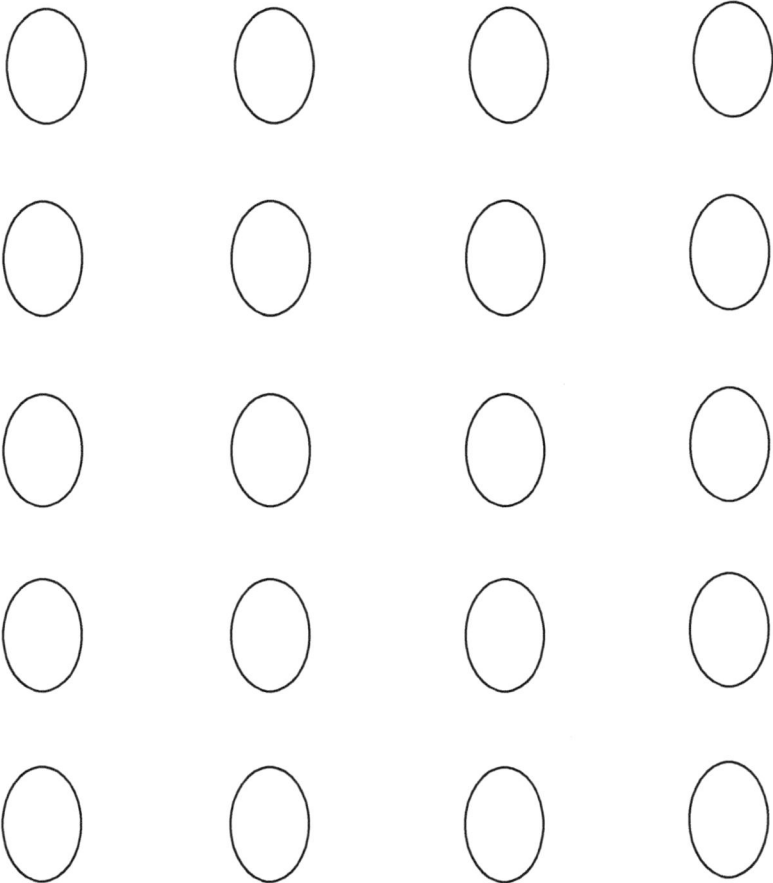

Step 2: *Scoring.* When the five minutes are up, answer the following questions to determine your preference for maximizing resources.

Range—How many circles did you use in your drawing?_____

Uniqueness—How many circles did you use to create different, original, or unusual ideas? _____

Subtotal for Range + Uniqueness _____

Agility—How many circles did you use to create different ideas, characters, or themes? _____

Enhancement—How many circles did you add additional detail to, so that they were more interesting, stronger, appealing, or complete?_____

Subtotal for Agility + Enhancement _____

Step 3: *Assessment*. Review your scores and notice in which areas you have used the most and least amount of circles. The descriptions below will further help you understand your natural tendency and preference for being innovative and using the resources you have available.

Range. If you created ideas using more than ten circles in this category, you have demonstrated the ability to easily generate ideas and alternate solutions to an issue. There is an implication here that you have an understanding of how to use the resources available to you through converting, defining, identifying, and predicting outcomes.

Uniqueness. If you created ideas using more than ten circles in this category, you have demonstrated the ability to produce ideas that are unusual or out of the ordinary. There is an implication here that you have an understanding of how to use the resources available to you through composing, integrating, modifying, reconstructing, and designing.

Range + Uniqueness = Divergent maximizer

Divergent maximizer. If the subtotal for your Range and Uniqueness scores is greater than 20, you are an innovative, divergent thinker who likely has the ability to produce a number of relevant and unusual ideas using the resources you have at hand.

Agility. If you created ideas using more than ten circles in this category, you have demonstrated the ability to produce ideas that show a variety of possibilities or realms of thought. There is an implication here that you have an understanding of how to use the resources available to you through envisioning ideas, predicting outcomes, enhancing concepts, and seeing things from a different point of view.

Enhancement. If you created ideas using more than ten circles in this category, you have demonstrated the ability to be reflective on a concept and enhance the end result through detail. There is an implication here that you place importance on format and content while having an understanding of how to use the resources available to you to evaluate and determine the best course of action.

Agility + Enhancement = Fusion maximizer

Fusion maximizer. If the subtotal for your Agility and Enhancement scores is greater than 20, you are a productive fusion thinker who likely has the ability to be motivated toward achieving results, capturing the essence of the information and resources involved, and knowing what is important.

If you scored lower than 10 in any of these categories, we recommend that you practice by using this exercise again and force yourself to be more creative or innovative. With practice, you will naturally begin to broaden your thinking and your subsequent capacity for innovation.

4

CHAMPION COMPETENCY #1

▲ Use Innovation Practices To Influence And Adjust ▼

The beginner scorns criticism. The wise soul carefully weighs it. And the Master says, "But, of course!"

MIKE DOOLEY
Notes from the Universe

Champions think outside the accepted inherent limitations of an issue and focus on innovation and adaptability as they constantly challenge the status quo. They incorporate innovative abilities to recover or adjust easily to misfortune or change. One frustrated leader once told us, "My team is having trouble thinking outside the box. Heck, they can't even agree on the size of the box, what materials the box should be constructed from, a reasonable budget for the box, or our first choice of box vendors! Oh yes, we are far from thinking 'outside' the box."

Think inside & outside the Box

Perhaps you have heard some of the negative comments made in the past about innovative ideas for the future of computers and telephones. Well-respected people forecasted how these innovations would influence the population. Noted quotes include:

"Computers in the future may weigh no more than 1.5 tons."— *Popular Mechanics,* forecasting the relentless march of science, 1949

"I think there is a world market for maybe five computers."— Thomas Watson, chairman of IBM, 1943

"This 'telephone' has too many shortcomings to be seriously considered as a means of communication. The device is inherently of no value to us."—Western Union internal memo, 1876

What a surprise these leaders would have if they read the 2011 Cisco report projecting "global Internet traffic to increase more than fourfold to 767 exabytes, or more than 3/4 of a Zettabyte, by 2014. This amount is 100 exabytes higher than the projected level in 2013, or an increase the equivalent of 10 times all the traffic traversing Internet Protocol networks in 2008. The nearly 64 exabytes of global IP traffic per month projected for 2014 is equivalent to 16 billion DVDs, 21 trillion MP3's, or 399 quadrillion text messages."

(Retrieved August 2, 2011 from http://www.cisco.com/web/MT/news/10/news_100610.html).

As for telephone users, in January 2011, "The number of mobile phone subscriptions reached the symbolic threshold of five billion," according to the secretary-general of the UN's International Telecommunications Union. (Retrieved August 2, 2011 http://nhne-pulse.org/2-08-billion-now-use-internet-5-28-billion-use-cell-phones). That is quite a different reality than Western Union predicted in 1876. Imagine if the company leaders saw the power of such devices as the 4G iPhone, and even that will soon be surpassed—by far. We want to stress that people see the world from their inherent vantage point, which then becomes their reality. When an ABL expands her thinking and takes a panoramic view of the situation/reality, the likelihood increases that a leader has to create a realistic and useful perspective and solution.

On the flip side, opinions and ideas of the past are not to be discarded too quickly. They can be used as innovative spring

Nothing is so OLD as the NEW

boards for the future. There is an old saying, "Where nothing is so old, as the new." Champions know how true this is. In 1908 Ford Motor Company's first car, the Model T, was designed to use ethanol (corn alcohol gasoline) as fuel. The project was cancelled for not being a viable design solution. The emergence of the concept of using ethanol as an "innovative" approach to the fuel crisis points to the adage, "Nothing is so old as the new."

AGILE ANALOGY

In 1965, visionary and cofounder of Intel, Gordon Moore, made a prediction that the number of transistors on a chip will double about every two years. Intel works with the developer community and customers to build platforms that combine elements such as microprocessors, chip sets, communications silicon, software, and other technologies. Moore wrote about the idea of transistors doubling every two years in his publication "Cramming More Components onto Integrated Circuits" (*Electronics Magazine*, 19 April 1965) Moore's innovative thinking has transpired into a commonly used term called "Moore's Law." His thinking has not only become part of Intel's mission, but has also held true for nearly forty years. As Intel's CEO Craig Barrett stated in 2005,

> We've used Moore's Law to drive the convergence of computing and communications. Intel's commitment to Moore's Law now allows us to create integrated platforms that deliver a broad range of capabilities for individuals and organizations that use technology. To realize the full potential of these capabilities, continued innovation and industry cooperation will be more important than ever. Innovation is driving the global digital economy. By working together as an industry and by advocating education and government policies that nurture innovation, there is no limit to what we can achieve. Multi-core technology provides the foundation for almost limitless innovation and creativity in addressing the changing ways people want to use computing and communications devices.

(Retrieved June 8, 2008 from
http://download.intel.com/museum/Moores_Law/Articles-Press_Releases/Press_Release_Mar2005.pdf).

Innovation seems to have endless possibilities if a person is open to thinking differently. Even within Intel and the computer community there is debate over the "conservativeness" of Moore's prediction. Now Intel is talking about "moving faster than Moore's Law." Innovative thought suggests a new version of Moore's Law. This new thinking believes performance of transistors will double every eighteen months and not every twenty-four months. Who knows what the next forty years will bring?

Leaders need to continually innovate their products, services, and processes. In our global, highly competitive world, becoming entrapped in commitment to a position and closing your mind to alternatives are no longer options. Innovative practices include

- Raising new questions.
- Viewing old problems from a new angle.
- Reacting quickly to changes in existing and potential markets.
- Generating alternatives that are also good for other people.

AGILE ILLSTRATION

To gain further insight on what it means for a leader to use innovative practices to influence and adjust, we went to Karl Schlatzer. We have worked with Karl in the past, helping him build a new product for WiMAX communications. WiMAX technology provides faster broadband wireless access covering larger areas for customers. Karl recognizes that the foundation of an ABL starts with a leader's character: "Everything else is built on that foundation. Character and the leader's capabilities are at the root of innovating and resolving issues, not technology as most would think."

Throughout his career, Karl has focused on using leadership to harness the capabilities of particular groups to form the technology that can be envisioned. He knows that, by getting a group to come together, and by using existing data, combined with relevance, you can leverage opportunities to drive business intelligence and arrive at an optimal and realistic decision for customers. His experience is a testament to this.

Currently, Karl is the executive in residence and director of global business development and channel sales at SAS Institute Inc. According to the SAS website, "SAS is the leader in business analytics software and services, and the largest independent vendor in the business intelligence market. With innovative business applications supported by an enterprise intelligence platform, SAS helps 44,000 organizations improve performance and deliver value by making better decisions faster." At SAS, Karl leverages the assets of third parties and the assets and resources of SAS to embed and deliver solutions to customers.

Before working at SAS, Karl was cofounder and chief marketing officer for GadgetSpace, a start-up that developed software and services that extended large-scale applications to wireless devices (for example, mobile phones and handheld computers like the BlackBerry, Palm Pilot, and the PocketPC).

Karl, along with the other founders, built GadgetSpace into a strong, successful company to the point that it was acquired by InPhonic, a wireless communications technology provider. InPhonic supplied equipment, software, and services to clients using mobile phones, handheld electronic organizers, and wireless email devices. Karl became the general manager of InPhonic and helped deliver "best-in-class" wireless solutions to customers, helped market WiMAX technology, and then moved on to SAS.

When we worked with Karl, we experienced his innovation and his practices, which were based on geographical, organizational, and occupational factors. This is how he led people to respond quickly to customers' needs and to building the business. He has a knack for helping organizations be resourceful when creating customer solutions to rising issues. When we asked Karl about his views on being an Agile Business Leader, it became very clear that his passion and belief for success revolve around the leader's character. Like us, Karl believes character is the underpinning of a Champion.

> Maybe I'm older and more cynical, but I really believe that the success and sustainability of an organization will not lie in its technology or the products and services it delivers; it will lie in the character of its leadership. If, in an effort to influence and adjust, the leader lacks integrity, the company will struggle. If the leader has a hard time determining how to do the "right thing" . . . the one that is best for the company and the customer and not necessarily for himself as the leader . . . the company will struggle. It's the leader who provides the organization with the resources of ideas, beliefs, and values significant to the business.

> We all see the world through different lenses and mental models. What is observed by me may not be observed by someone else. In my work I have to be resourceful and understand how to translate things for it to make sense to everyone involved.

> Leaders in organizations work from two lenses. The first lens focuses on the roles and responsibilities of the leader

and the types of specific knowledge that must be acquired to make the business succeed. The second lens focuses on the culture and history of the organization and how decisions and relationships will be created and executed. These two lenses continually interact in combination with the character of the leader to push the elements that are most important and assist a leader in becoming a Champion.

You can't outsource the traits of a Champion. Champions have a strong moral basis and have the strong ability to galvanize people around a cause. They create the corporate solidarity, the institution of value, and the condition of order. This means ABLs can identify the cause and work with a purpose to innovate and achieve results. If they *cannot* do this, then they are not leaders and they are just passing time.

As I see it, a true leader must be willing to consistently remove personal impact and ego from decision making and innovative action. This is very difficult as (a) human nature is what it is and (b) almost by definition, our metrics as assigned by the organization are designed to be "personal" performance measurements.

A natural and understandable inclination, then, will be to behave in a way (while prioritizing and directing) to optimize personal performance measurements, and not necessarily to altruistically operate for the greater good of other employees, of customers, of investors. . . . As the leader, the person uses innovative practices to influence and adjust for optimum results.

ABLs have the integrity and the ability to do the right thing even when it is not self-serving. The leader is the person who has the strength to encourage people to move toward taking the proverbial "hill." Some leaders put a lot of emphasis on innovation and not so much on execution, which can be a fatal flaw. The leader has to suspend any negative beliefs or assumptions to reach a solution while legitimizing certain beliefs and values to superimpose them onto the current reality.

Leaders need to generate a shared sense of mission and cause with people, so everyone can move toward the common vision. This is true because when people say, "I don't know where my 'hill' is," then people will begin to think they might have to go off and create or innovate in the direction of their own "hill." Not innovating a shared mission can cause chaos within the organization.

It's a leader's character that drives people to follow, and they follow because ABL Champions hold themselves to a higher set of standards. They have a set of ideals they strive for, and those ideals are formed on the basis of character with the foundation of integrity, and trust. The ABL with' character also has strength, integrity, and a strong sense of purpose. If a leader does not have a strong character, then he will not succeed. Oh, he might get promoted, but in the end he will leave wreckage throughout the organization, and that is not my definition of success. Integrity and character provide the foundation for a leader. They are *the* requirements for successful leadership. Many skills and traits identified in the ABL model can be learned, refined, or "compensated for"—but integrity and character need to be "core" to the individual.

Arguably, the financial mess in 2008 offers a brilliant example of why the ability to disassociate from personal gain and incorporate the concept of leadership having innate character and integrity as a foundation is so critical. During the financial crisis there were end-to-end failures to do what was right (for borrowers, institutions, stockholders, and the country) vs. pursuit of short-term achievement (personal gain) for individuals in the banking/lending food chain. The result of this building or compounding self-interest by those in leadership roles was and is systemic failure and collapse. Ultimately, character/integrity (when paired with action) leads to credibility and the ability to influence others and adjust your course of action. Credibility (or trust) is the currency of business—internal to the organization or in external interactions. It is the ability to enable employees (or customers or partners) to have faith and confidence in the leader's decisions. Employees must know that the leader's decisions are "right" for the moment or for the longer term. Their directives are given in everyone's best interest and in the context of something greater than the leader.

I've seen a lot of people who have false success, basically because they have a false facade. The person might have ninety days of success, but that is really no different than constructing a Hollywood prop. They are fakes as leaders and have no sustainable character. At the end of the day, I know I have won at being a good leader when I go home and feel like I have done the right thing and the enterprise as a whole has improved. Then I know I have done my job. I see the lights of understanding turn on in people's minds, and they begin to get enthusiastic and excited about doing the job we need to accomplish. When my people become passionate about a cause, then I have led them well.

It's how you communicate your message that causes people to get excited enough to move. The point to remember is that the type of communication you use needs to be different for everyone. As a leader, you have to know what will be the best way for you to influence the situation. A leader needs the ability to communicate well, paint pictures, and get people to understand why they need to act and move in the direction they need to go. The leader must communicate context and convert it into a higher sense of purpose and an understanding of how people will benefit, if they follow that direction. If I cannot get people to understand and translate the information I've given them about the purpose and what needs to be done, then it won't happen. You have to provide a nirvana sense of leadership. By that I mean to make it interesting, exciting, and relevant to the person. You have to be able to get people to move toward the objective you have set.

Tied into having good communication skills is the point that leaders can't be introverted and never looking out into the world. Every day, all of us are saturated with information, emails, and news flashes. It's more difficult these days to communicate as a leader because your message has to get through all the information clutter that people are managing. An ABL has to be a strong communicator and have strong communication processes. I have to remember that whatever level I'm at, others will receive continuous and constant communication from me. I know that if my communication is not relevant and specific, it will be dismissed because there is a competing, mind-saturating amount of information floating around out there. My nanosecond of important communication in their lives must not get lost in the clouds. If I walk into a meeting well prepared and make a point in the first few seconds, I will face less resistance. If my written and verbal communication is combined with empathic, concise, and relevant information that addresses the higher purpose of the project, I will begin to see results. The message I give speaks to "here's the 'hill,' and here's what you can do to achieve our objective in the sea of information and competing forces." You have to be good at this as a leader, or your message will get lost.

There is always a lot of opportunity for mind clutter when communicating to others. That is why an ABL must:

- Focus on decision-making and communication styles related to the decision-making process.
- Form plans for executing the mission.
- Create objectives aligned to the mission.
- Communicate the elements of the plan to each person involved and tell them what they can expect from the end result.
- Build upon the strength of each person to accomplish the goal.
- Clarify who is in charge, with no ambiguity around this point.
- Be execution centric.

I know that I not only have to influence and adjust to achieve increased revenues; I also deal with individual variables, organizational variables, and technological variables while leading within the organization. Dealing with all these different variables can be hard for a leader. It's like getting a bunch of magnetic filings all going in one direction. It's a hard "to do."

One of the companies I worked for, InPhonic, later collapsed and declared bankruptcy. This happened long after I left. There were many failures of leadership, but the most preventable or repairable were the unethical business practices, many of which emanated from or were endorsed by senior management. During my tenure, there was little evidence of a do-what's-right mentality—resulting in a company that (at its core) viewed business partners and customers solely as a means to an end and lacked any sense of moral responsibility beyond consummating a transaction. Personal excellence was not valued, fear was an acceptable management technique, and the organization simply lacked a soul. This is not to say that all employees were of a similar mind-set; InPhonic was populated with some truly good people, many of whom tried to execute to high standards in their sphere. But the tone that was set at an institutional level conspired against "the right thing" in day-to-day practice—and ultimately, this was not a happy place to be. InPhonic acquired GadgetSpace from me and the other founders. During the first visit to our new owners at InPhonic, the GadgetSpace principals were shocked at the vibe of the organization. For several years, we firewalled off our (acquired) division from the corporate challenges of InPhonic, and we were able to maintain a positive (if sometimes strained) environment within our sphere of control.

Agile leadership can flourish only if a proper environment is established, with measurements that reward longer-term horizons, encourage a holistic view of the business, cross-link the interests of the management team(s), and reinforce and celebrate ethical behavior. Ideally, all levels in the hierarchy need to have a do-the-right-thing mind-set, and organizational hiring policies and actions must emphasize and value the correct traits.

In my current role and throughout my career, I have learned to develop relationships of mutual under-standing and confirm that the chosen technology is organizationally valid and can be implemented. For implementation to occur, you must be able to influence and adjust in order to deliver promises made to the customer.

The ABL Champion's hallmark is an inquiring mind, one that not only innovates but is also receptive and has an attitude of expectancy. I know I have done my job as an ABL when I act in good character to assist people in internalizing the purpose, accepting the mission, and acting with passion toward the cause. Then I know we will not have a problem developing innovative practices, and we can influence customers as we adjust to their needs.

Three variables impact innovative practices and implementation.

1. *Individual variables:* How people think, their personality, their decision-making styles, how they expect they will contribute to the cause, and most important, their character.

2. *Organizational variables:* The culture of the organization, the autonomy the business unit has, the reward system, the power distribution, how central operations are, and what behaviors are accepted with the organization.

3. *Technological variables:* The type of technology being used and the components, reliability, diversity, and transferability of the technology.

As part of my capabilities to innovate and implement, I have to be agile and focus in two directions, both internal and external. I have to determine the most effective and efficient means to market our business.

Internally, I focus on legal, finance, product marketing, and communication factors. I have to make sure all of these elements are aligned.

- Externally, I have to focus on a wild idea and make sure it is valuable to the customer. I have to take into account different companies and foci and bring them all together and map how to deliver a wonderful result to customers.

I try to figure out and exploit everybody's motivations and assets. This has to be done tactically, strategically, and with the greatest of integrity.

In one situation, we had a 3-billion-customer company come to us with a different mind-set than ours. They wanted to generate business through a partnership with us. They were thinking of a joint development, one we hadn't considered. The combination of two companies' assets would change the technology game and, in so doing, blow open market opportunities. We saw it as a good partnership. It took six to twelve months of continuous interaction, building greater degrees of trust and forming cultural understandings before everyone involved would realize we were creating commitment. It started with a suspicion—"It seems like this is good"—and moved to multiple interactions: "I think we can do business together." Finally, we established trust and commitment. The project only accelerated when there was a comfortable feeling and we had trust between both parties.

The capacity of a leader to use his character to build trust exhibits and exudes the traits of the Champion. You manage down but you exude up in order to get people on board. But the more I think about the ABL model, the more I realize that integrity and character are the foundation and *the* requirement for successful leadership. Many skills and traits identified in the ABL model can be learned, refined, or compensated for, but this role of Champion needs to be core to the involved individual.

The leaders we talk to consistently speak about how the risks and demands placed on them have increased. Some are frustrated because they feel like they lack the time to make a detailed analysis of a dangerous situation and have even less time to respond to situations in an innovative way. These leaders are anxious because they must make rapid decisions and accept the subsequent consequences for their actions. Being innovative in these time-pressured moments of decision making is difficult. These same leaders say, "When it comes to the inconsequential decisions, it's easy, I might flip a coin: heads is yes and tails is no. But when my or someone else's life is on the line, and I have to innovate a solution and make a decision in a short period of time, I resort to using my primary instinct."

The primary instinct that these leaders are talking about is intuition, and it is commonly used for survival. Intuition is the purest form of instinct. In our experience, the leaders who are innovative also use their intuition as part of their thought processes, because intuition helps a leader respond to situations independent of experience or reason.

There is a lot of interesting research on intuition. Intuition has been described as learned expertise, imaginative thinking, a venturesome personality, and intrinsic motivation or working in a creative environment. In the past it was thought that intuition or "acute perceptions, precognition, and ingenious wisdom" occurred when you used your instincts, intelligence, and orientation in unison. Einstein said, "One of the most valuable factors in life is intuition." In the Buddhist faith, intuition is considered "intellectual light." In Latin, the word for intuition is related to having a keen vision or insight. There are lots of variables and thoughts on the concept of having and using your intuition, but at its core, intuition is the natural ability not found at a conscious level. Intelligence can only analyze; intuition is the absolute in brain power. It is the result of the right and left hemispheres of the brain working in unison so that a person can create a solution without knowing all the details. Intuition is when individuals use their brain along with all the skills and abilities they have to form the basis of making choices and obtaining insights.

In the Myers-Briggs Type Indicator personality test, based on the work of Carl Jung, only 25 percent of the general population reports a preference for intuition. The other 75 percent prefer immediate, real, solid facts and are not often inspired. In many studies, successful leaders of organizations are typically found to have a preference for intuition when tested. It is odd that for something that is so natural, intuition is not the style of choice. Perhaps the reason is that intuition isn't easily proven or justified. It is often discounted as an unexplained thought rather than a keen perception.

AGILE ILLUSTRATION

Intuition has an important place in the role of the Agile Business Leader. If everything had to first make logical sense, the world might never have seen the light bulb, the telephone, or the Internet. Eileen had an opportunity to meet with Larry Roberts in March 2001 while doing human resource work with him. Larry is considered to be "the father of the Internet." In 1966 he was the director and innovator of ARPAnet, the first data exchange over a network. This exchange occurred between computers at UCLA and Stanford

University. It wasn't an easy sell to get these two universities to work together because everyone wanted to protect their own work. Once Larry got them to think in a more agile way and consider the possibilities of jointly publishing papers, sharing research, and connecting like they had never done before, everyone wanted to have access to the opportunity. Larry also has a knack for being a good salesman.

Eileen asked Larry, "As an innovator and leader, what do you see is next for the Internet?"

He said, "We haven't even begun to see its possibilities. I knew creating this technology was a good thing. But now we are expecting very old technology to work and support applications like voice and video, and that is a stretch. I dream about bigger, better, and faster networks happening in the future. My intuition knows this is the direction we need to move toward. We will not recognize the Internet of the future."

VISUALIZING A NEW WORLD

Agile Business Leaders rely on intuition, along with logic, to take their companies and ideas to the leading edge. Nobody who rises to a high level in an organization does it without the use of intuition. The brilliant few who run the organization are there because they have the instinct and brainpower to do it. Agile Business Leaders understand the value and advantage of using intuition and will use it as a spark to lead to success through thought and discovery.

We emphasize the importance of intuition in this book because it has been shown that leaders who develop superior insight through intuition are enabled to perceive whole situations in sudden leaps of logic. John Mihalasky and Douglas Dean at the New Jersey Institute of Technology discovered that 80 percent of the CEOs whose profits doubled over a five-year period had above-average intuitive powers. Many CEOs even acknowledged a private belief in ESP, based not on the scientific literature or an acquaintance with psychics, but because they'd seen its presence in their own lives. Mihalasky and Dean point out that the two basic principles of intuition are

1. It must be developed. People should strive to be aware of their intuition on a daily basis.
2. You must combine intuition with reason. Effective creative conceptualization is required when one incorporates reason and logic as well as intuition and feeling.

(Retrieved September 19, 2011, from http://www.fsbmedia.com/article_display.php?article_id=739)

There is a potency to intuition. Intuitive information processing can improve efficiency when a leader takes all the accumulated collective experience and knowledge he has and transforms it into an idea or solution. Leaders who rely solely on intuition are also prone to predictable errors and misjudgments. Unfortunately, with remarkable ease, a leader using only his intuition can form and sustain false beliefs. In some cases, leaders begin to have delusions of grandeur, possibly from feeding on the power of their intuition.

When you hear an ABL say, "*Aha!*" that's often the sound of intuition meeting innovation: "AAHHhhaa!" and "This is a stellar idea!"

Innovation helps Champions with decisions that involve exploration of new terrains. It contributes to their ability to reach first-mover advantage and create a competitive space for the business.

For the Agile Business Leader, situations involving risk and uncertainty are the ones where intuition is most often used. Some people say that the Golden Rule should be, "There is no right way and no wrong way, so take the way you get."

Intuition helps the Champion be innovative and confident, and to go boldly where no one else has gone. Intuition and innovation are strongly balanced between bravery and caution. They give the Champion the ability to deal with ambiguity, implausibility, and uncertainty, and result in the Champion thinking and saying, "I can do that!" The Champion knows that by logic we prove, and by intuition we discover.

The secret to ABLs using innovative and intuitive practices is that they are relatively free of emotional disturbances—like obsessions, compulsions, phobias, and unresolved, emotionally traumatic experiences. The Champion simply dissociates from using only logical or linear thinking. She allows both the left brain (logic-focused, rational thought) and the right brain (intuition-focused and matters of the heart) to be fully engaged and interacting while embracing the role of Champion.

AGILE ILLUSTRATION

At a UN speech given by Israeli Prime Minister Benjamin Netanyahu in 2010, he described his confidence in the future with a commonly held assumption that the history of telecommunications and microelectronic development will predict the development trajectory of a low-carbon/sustainable energy future. The following excerpt is from that speech:

> The primitivism of the ninth century ought to be no match for the progress of the twenty-first century. The allure of freedom, the power of technology, the reach of communications should surely win the day. Ultimately, the past cannot triumph over the future. And the future offers all nations magnificent bounties of hope. The pace of progress is growing exponentially. It took us centuries to get from the printing press to the telephone, decades to get from the telephone to the personal computer, and only a few years to get from the personal computer to the Internet.
>
> What seemed impossible a few years ago is already outdated, and we can scarcely fathom the changes that are yet to come. We will crack the genetic code. We will cure the incurable. We will lengthen our lives. We will find a cheap alternative to fossil fuels and clean up the planet. Over seventy years ago, Winston Churchill lamented what he called the "confirmed unteachability of mankind," the unfortunate habit of civilized societies to sleep until danger nearly overtakes them. Churchill bemoaned what he called the "want of foresight, the unwillingness to act when action will be simple and effective, the lack of clear thinking, and the confusion of counsel until emergency comes, until self-preservation strikes its jarring gong." I speak here today in the hope that Churchill's assessment of the "unteachability of mankind" is for once proven wrong.

(Retrieved December 9, 2011 from
http://www.al-bab.com/arab/docs/pal/netanyahu20110923.htm)

Prime Minister Netanyahu's hope was that we could all learn from history and prevent danger in the future. At the time of his speech, however, Israelis did not have confidence in their leadership. Citizens believed that the leadership was incompetent. Netanyahu continued to present his beliefs on what type of future the country could create and the importance of using innovation while acting and thinking about moving forward.

With innovation, small thoughts can be converted into very large results. We have all seen and experienced innovation boosting performance and improving security, reliability, and manageability. The next Theory in Practice Activity presents a tool to help leaders tap into the best innovative approaches for a leader's preference and assist in making leaders' minds more agile.

THEORY IN PRACTICE ACTIVITY 3.2

INNOVATE

Objective of this exercise: To assist in generating new or alternative innovative ideas to support and produce divergent thinking for your product or service lines. The INNOVATE tool can be used to ignite innovation and help resolve challenges.

Instructions: Follow the steps 1-4

Step 1: Describe the challenge requiring innovative thinking.

Step 2: Define requirements that all ideas/solutions must meet.

Step 3: Use the table below and the acronym INNOVATE to create or modify product or service lines.

INNOVATE			
		Definition	**Prompting Questions**
I	**Import**	Bring from a foreign or external source, transfer from one format to another, usually within a new file.	1. What resources from other countries can we use? 2. What other industries' services or products can we import to improve our offerings? 3. What external sources do we need to access to improve delivery?
N	**Nano It**	Dealing with the smallest parts of matter that we can manipulate, the ability to devise and develop materials and devices on an atomic and molecular scale, materials reduced	1. How can we use nano-technology to improve delivery mechanisms or produce products and services more quickly and efficiency? 2. How can we add real value to our products and services to enable the creation of a whole new product or

			to the nanoscale can suddenly show very different properties compared to what they exhibit.	service line? 3. What new architectures can we design to improve functionality, performance, or operations?
N	**Niche**		A position well suited for the product or service where its status in the environment or community affects its survival.	1. What market or service area can we expand into that is currently not being served? 2. How can we define a different role for our product or service, thus creating a new niche? 3. How can our products and services be more unique, resourceful, and attractive?
O	**Obliterate**		Erase, blot out, remove from existence, and destroy utterly all trace or significance of.	1. What can we remove from a product or service to enhance its value? 2. What can we remove from a product or service without losing profit or performance? 3. How else can we achieve the solution without the normal way of doing it?
V	**Viral**		Quickly and widely spread or popularize.	1. How can we ensure that we are tapping into all media sources to have our message go viral? 2. How can our message be unique, resourceful, and attractive? 3. How can we improve our message so that it is easy to

			understand, easy to share, and includes a social imperative?
A	**Accelerate**	Cause to move faster, hasten the progress or development of, and bring about at an earlier time.	1. How can we greatly accelerate what we are already doing? 2. How can we put our products and services to a different use to accelerate our profits? 3. How can change what we are currently doing to lower production costs?
T	**Technology Refresh**	Strengthen and replenish, restore or maintain by renewing supply, update or renew.	1. How could new materials or equipment change the nature of our products and services? 2. What materials, features, processes, people, products, or components can we add or improve upon? 3. How can we incorporate new technology to include more intelligence and flexibility than we could possibly design into our products and services?
E	**Extend**	Stretch out to its fullest capacity, cause it to be or perform longer, and increase the scope, meaning, or application of.	1. What modifications can be made for our products and services to function at their fullest capacity? 2. How can we expand what is already being offered in the industry? 3. How can our product and service lines become household names?

Step 4: Prioritize ideas and identify action steps.

Champions have an intellectual curiosity and are motivated to develop new solutions to improve business operations. They know that when it comes to innovation, timing is everything. Champions have the thinking style, cognitive development, and life experiences to succeed. They raise new questions, view old problems from a new angle, react quickly to changes in existing and potential markets, and generate alternatives that are also good for other people. In essence, Champions know how to be resourceful by using innovative practices to influence and adjust.

5

CHAMPION COMPETENCY #2

▲ Build Internal and External Networks ▼

Champions know that ideas and solutions can be blocked because they have failed to reach the right people, for the purposes of broadening their perspective and gaining input on their thinking. Champions construct their network through relatively high-stakes activities that bring them into contact with diverse groups of people. They purposefully build their network by choosing the "right" individuals to associate with and, from that network, from whom they can become informed.

On January 22, 2007, Craig Barrett, chairman and former CEO of Intel Corporation, gave a speech before the National Higher Education Leadership Summit. During his remarks, he pointed to the importance of international competitiveness and three key aspects involved in becoming a business champion:

> Number one is education. You have to have an educated workforce. Number two is you have to have ideas for the next generation of products, services, and companies. That's where basic investment and research and development are important. Number three is you have to have an environment where smart people get together with smart ideas and do something. But none of that has a chance to begin unless you have smart people. And that's why education is always the number-one priority.

(Retrieved December 9, 2011 from
http://www.biztools4schools.org/hear_from_business_leaders_who
_champion_education)

Building an internal and external network helps Champions educate themselves by

- Locating individuals with expertise.
- Discovering others with similar experiences and interests.
- Locating tools and ideas already developed.
- Forming relationships for future development.
- Creating a "safe place" for asking sensitive questions or practicing skills that are not fully formed.
- Identifying outside influences that can help spark new ideas and solutions.

One approach a Champion uses for increasing his education and enhancing learning is participating in communities of practice. Communities of practice, or CoP, are emerging as a key element to learning and expanding one's network. Etienne Wenger and Jean Lave are the most well-known and respected experts when it comes to coining the phrase communities of practice and initially defining the term in the 1990s. Wenger and Lave believed that communities of practice are everywhere and that most people are usually involved in one or more—whether at work, school, or home, or in civic or leisure activities. In some groups we are core members; in others we are more at the margins.* Communities of practice have been around for as long as human beings have learned together, and we travel through numerous communities over the course of our lives.

*The discussion of communities of practice is adapted with permission of Etienne Wegner.

Communities of practice are not called that in all organizations. Some might be called learning networks, thematic groups, or tech clubs. Some are small, and some can be very large. Some are local, and some cover the globe. Some meet mainly face-to-face; some mostly online. Some are within an organization, and some include members from various organizations. Some are formally recognized, often supported with a budget; some are completely informal and even invisible.

In fact, communities of practice are everywhere. They are a familiar experience, so familiar that they often escape our attention. Yet when such a community is given a name and brought into focus, it becomes a perspective that can help us understand our world better. In particular, it allows us to see past more obvious formal structures, such as organizations, classrooms, or nations, and per-

ceive the structures defined by engagement in practice and the informal learning that comes with it.

Communities of practice are formed by people who engage in a
process of collective learning in a shared domain of human endeavor: a tribe learning to survive, a band of artists seeking new
forms of expression, a group of engineers working on similar problems, a clique of pupils defining their identity in the school, a network of surgeons exploring novel techniques, a gathering of first-
time managers helping each other cope.

The Characteristics of Communities of Practice

Communities of practice are groups of people who share a concern
or a passion for something they do and learn how to do it better as
they interact regularly. Note that this definition allows for, but does
not assume, intentionality: learning can be the reason the community comes together or an incidental outcome of member's' interactions. Not everything called a community is a community of

practice. A neighborhood, for instance, is often called a community, but is usually not a community of practice.

Three characteristics are crucial in having a community of practice. The combination of these three elements constitutes a community of practice, and by developing these three elements in parallel, one cultivates such a community.

1. **The domain**. A community of practice is not merely a club of friends or a network of connections between people. It has an identity defined by a shared domain of interest. Membership therefore implies a commitment to the domain, and therefore a shared competence that distinguishes members from other people. (You could belong to the same network as someone and never know it.) The domain is not necessarily something recognized as expertise outside the community. A youth gang may have developed all sorts of ways of dealing with their domain: surviving on the street and maintaining some kind of identity. They value their collective competence and learn from each other, even though few people outside the group may value or even recognize their expertise.

2. **The community.** In pursuing their interest in their domain, members engage in joint activities and discussions, help each other, and share information. They build relationships that enable them to learn from each other. A website in itself is not a community of practice. Having the same job or the same title does not make for a community of practice unless members interact and learn together. The claims processors in a large insurance company or students in U.S. high schools may have much in common, yet unless they interact and learn together, they do not form a community of practice. But members of a community of practice do not necessarily work together on a daily basis. The Impressionists, for instance, used to meet in cafes and studios to discuss the style of

painting they were inventing together. These interactions were essential to making them a community of practice even though they often painted alone.

3. **The practice.** A community of practice is not merely a community of interest—people who like certain kinds of movies, for instance. Members of a community of practice are practitioners. They develop a shared repertoire of resources: experiences, stories, tools, and ways of addressing recurring problems—in short, a shared practice. This takes time and sustained interaction. A good conversation with a stranger on an airplane may give you all sorts of interesting insights, but it does not in itself make for a community of practice. The development of a shared practice may be more or less self-conscious. The windshield-wiper engineers at an auto manufacturer make a concerted effort to collect and document the tricks and lessons they have learned into a knowledge base. In contrast, nurses who meet regularly for lunch in a hospital cafeteria may not realize that their lunch discussions are one of their main sources of knowledge about how to care for patients. Still, in the course of all these conversations, the people have developed a set of stories and cases that have become a shared repertoire for their practice.

Relationships, Identity, and Shared Interests and Repertoire

A community of practice involves much more than the technical knowledge or skill associated with undertaking some task. Members are involved in a set of relationships over time, and communities develop around things that matter to people. The fact that they are organizing around some particular area of knowledge and activity gives members a sense of joint enterprise and identity. For a community of practice to function, it needs to generate and appropriate a shared repertoire of ideas, commitments, and memories. It also needs to develop various resources such as tools, documents, routines, vocabulary, and symbols that in some way carry the accumulated knowledge of the community. In other words, it involves practice: ways of doing and approaching things that members share to some significant extent.

The interactions involved, and the ability to undertake larger or more complex activities and projects though cooperation, bind people together and help to facilitate relationship and trust. Communities of practice can be seen as self-organizing systems and have many of the benefits and characteristics of associational life, such as the generation of what Robert Putnam and others have discussed as social capital.

What Do Communities of Practice Look Like?

Communities develop their practice through a variety of activities. The following list provides a few typical examples:

Problem solving: "Can we work on this design and brainstorm some ideas? I'm stuck."

Requests for information: "Where can I find the code to connect to the server?"

Seeking experience: "Has anyone dealt with a customer in this situation?"

Reusing assets: "I have a proposal for a local area network I wrote for a client last year. I can send it to you, and you can easily tweak it for this new client."

Coordination and synergy: "Can we combine our purchases of solvent to achieve bulk discounts?"

Discussing developments: "What do you think of the new CAD system? Does it really help?"

Documentation projects: "We have faced this problem five times now. Let us write it down once and for all."

Visits: "Can we come and see your after-school program? We need to establish one in our city."

Mapping knowledge and identifying gaps: "Who knows what, and what are we missing? What other groups should we connect with?"

Where Is the Concept Being Applied?

The concept of community of practice has found a number of practical applications in business, organizational design, government, education, professional associations, development projects, and civic life.

Organizations. The concept has been adopted most readily by people in business because of the recognition that knowledge is a critical asset that needs to be managed strategically. Initial efforts at managing knowledge had focused on information systems, with disappointing results. Communities of practice provided a new approach, which focused on people and on the social structures that enable them to learn with and from each other. Today, just about every organization of a reasonable size has some communities-of-practice initiative. A number of characteristics explain this rush of interest in communities of practice as a vehicle for developing strategic capabilities in organizations:

- Communities of practice enable practitioners to take collective responsibility for managing the knowledge they need, recognizing that, given the proper structure, they are in the best position to do so.

- Communities among practitioners create a direct link between learning and performance, because the same people participate in communities of practice and in teams and business units.

- Practitioners can address the tacit and dynamic aspects, as well as the more explicit aspects, of knowledge creation and sharing.

- Communities are not limited by formal structures: they create connections among people across organizational and geographic boundaries.

From this perspective, the knowledge of an organization lives in a constellation of communities of practice, each taking care of a specific aspect of the competence that the organization needs. However, the very characteristics that make communities of practice a good fit for stewarding knowledge—autonomy, practitioner orientation, informality, crossing boundaries—are also characteristics that make them a challenge for traditional hierarchical organizations. How this challenge is going to affect these organizations remains to be seen.

Government. Like businesses, government organizations face knowledge challenges of increasing complexity and scale. They have adopted communities of practice for much the same reason, though the formality of the bureaucracy can come in the way of open knowledge sharing. Beyond internal communities, typical government problems such as education, health, and security require coordination and knowledge sharing across levels of government. There also, communities of practice hold the promise of enabling connections among people across formal structures. Even so, there are substantial organizational issues to overcome.

Education. Schools and districts are organizations in their own right, and they also face increasing knowledge challenges. The first applications of communities of practice have been in teacher training and in providing isolated administrators with access to colleagues. There is a wave of interest in these peer-to-peer professional-development activities. But in the education sector, learning is not only a means to an end: it is the end product. The perspective of communities of practice is therefore also relevant at this level. In business, focusing on communities of practice adds a layer of complexity to the organization, but it does not fundamentally change what the business is about. In schools, changing learning theory or approach is a much deeper transformation that inevitably takes longer. The perspective of communities of practice affects educational practices along three dimensions:

- *Internally.* How to organize educational experiences that ground school learning in practice through participation in communities around subject matters?

- *Externally.* How to connect the experience of students to actual practice through peripheral forms of participation in broader communities beyond the walls of the school?

- *Over the lifetime of students.* How to serve the lifelong learning needs of students by organizing communities of practice focused on topics of continuing interest to students beyond the initial schooling period?

From this perspective, the school is not the privileged locus of learning. It is not a self-contained, closed world in which students acquire knowledge to be applied outside, but is part of a broader learning system. The class is not the primary learning event; life itself is the main learning event. Schools, classrooms, and training sessions still have a role to play in this vision, but they have to be in the service of the learning that happens in the world.

Associations. A growing number of associations, professional and otherwise, are seeking ways to focus on learning through reflection on practice. Their members are restless, and their allegiance is fragile. They need to offer high-value learning activities. The peer-to-peer learning activities typical of communities of practice offer a complementary alternative to more traditional course offerings and publications.

Social sector. In the civic domain, there is an emergent interest in building communities among practitioners. In the nonprofit world, for instance, foundations are recognizing that philanthropy needs to focus on learning systems in order to fully leverage funded projects. But practitioners are seeking peer-to-peer connections and learning opportunities with or without the support of institutions. This includes regional economic development, with intraregional communities on various domains, as well as interregional learning with communities gathering practitioners from various areas.

International development. The challenge for developing nations relates as much to knowledge as finances. A number of people believe that a communities-of-practice approach can provide a new paradigm for development work. It emphasizes knowledge building among practitioners. Some development agencies now see their role as conveners of such communities, rather than as providers of knowledge.

The Web. Technologies such as the Internet have extended the reach of our interactions beyond the geographical limitations of traditional communities, but the increase in flow of information does not obviate the need for community. In fact, increased information flow expands the possibilities for community and calls for new kinds of communities based on shared practice.

The concept of community of practice is influencing theory and practice in many domains. From its humble beginnings in apprenticeship studies, the concept was grabbed by businesses interested in knowledge management and has progressively found its way into other sectors. It has now become the foundation of a perspective on knowing and learning that informs efforts to create learning systems in various sectors and at various levels of scale, from local communities to single organizations, partnerships, cities, regions, and the entire world.

(Retrieved September 17, 2001 from:

http://www.ewenger.com/theory and included in this book with permission from Etienne Wenger) Etienne Wenger has recognized the process that CoPs tend to work through, as shown in the graphic detailing a CoP's stages of development.

Stages of Development

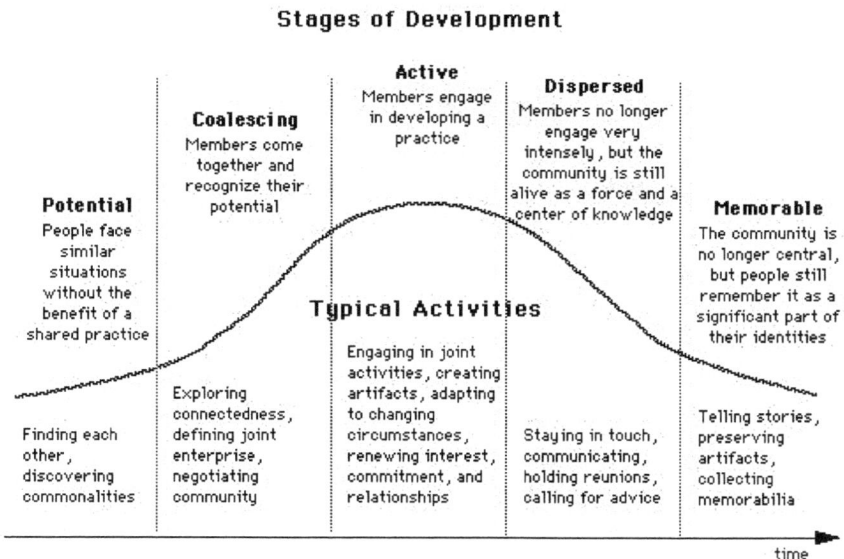

Potential	Coalescing	Active	Dispersed	Memorable
People face similar situations without the benefit of a shared practice	Members come together and recognize their potential	Members engage in developing a practice	Members no longer engage very intensely, but the community is still alive as a force and a center of knowledge	The community is no longer central, but people still remember it as a significant part of their identities

Typical Activities

| | | Engaging in joint activities, creating artifacts, adapting to changing | | |
| Finding each other, discovering commonalities | Exploring connectedness, defining joint enterprise, negotiating community | circumstances, renewing interest, commitment, and relationships | Staying in touch, communicating, holding reunions, calling for advice | Telling stories, preserving artifacts, collecting memorabilia |

time

Champions know that the practice of opening up to different trains of thought can lead to doing things differently and becoming more agile. In the role of Champion, leaders promote and engage in these communities of practice to positively influence business performance. They use technologies such as blogs, wikis, and virtual real-time conversations as the emerging tools for communities to gather and share knowledge and reach the goal of bringing out the community's own internal direction, character, and energy.

AGILE ILLUSTRATION

In one of Eileen's communities of practice, she met with a group of other businesswomen, all from very diverse backgrounds. This section relates Eileen's experience.

> One community of practice we were involved in personally included leaders from small businesses who wanted a way to develop and grow their businesses. The group met once a month, and the format was simple. Each leader had five minutes to make a presentation about the status of her busi-

ness, and then the group had ten minutes to ask thought-provoking questions, offer suggestions for improving the leader's course of action, or link up someone from their network to help this business leader.

This was one of the most diverse groups of people we had ever convened. One leader was an accountant, another ran a business dealing with elder care, another was a graphic designer, another worked with those designing parks and facilities for the disabled population, one had a recruiting company; we focused on organizational development. We remember some months dragging ourselves to the meeting, thinking it was just one more thing on our to-do list, only to find that it was the most stimulating and beneficial event we had attended all month, and our motivation to build the business increased even more because of the new ideas received from our network.

Our mission was to challenge, support, and grow as service providers and business leaders. As a group of women business owners, our vision was for our meetings to offer clarity in direction and value in each other's diverse thinking. Together we would serve as an executive committee to each other's businesses and coach each other toward better business performance.

Our meetings were very formatted and efficient. They were two hours long, and not a minute was wasted. We all valued time and recognized that committing to two hours of time when we could be out doing our own business development was time to be used wisely. As part of the process, leaders prepared a very simple report containing a few bullet points to use as talking points for the five-minute presentation (see form). Each person had five minutes to present her Community of Practice Business Update. This presentation was followed by an open forum for fifteen minutes where others in the group could ask questions, make suggestions for improvement, provide resources from their own network or call the person to account because she promised to complete an action for their business last month and the task had not yet been completed. There was a hard stop at the end of fifteen minutes, and we moved on to the next person. If a conversation needed to continue, an alternative time was arranged.

This might sound too structured and controlled. I will pass along this advice: if you have six people in a room who are going to talk about themselves or give advice to others, appoint a timekeeper. I am a firm believer that a task will take as much time as it is given. For this reason the group all agreed to stay within these times, and throughout our two years together we never had any issues. Nor did we ever use a timer or alarm. We simply had a timekeeper say, "We have one minute left," "The time is up," and the group moved on to the next person.

We present this format to you on the following pages in the hope that you might be able to make use of it and find it beneficial in your own community of practice.

Community of Practice Business Update

Area of Accountability

Last Month's Plan_____

_____

_____

_____

Trend or Drivers for Your Industry

_____

_____

_____

Networking Activities/Results

_____

_____

_____

Marketing Activities/Results for the Company

_____

_____

_____

Developmental Activities for You

_____

_____

_____

Economic Accomplishments

_____

_____

_____

Personal Accomplishments

_____
_____
_____

Successes and Celebrations

_____
_____
_____

Short-Term Actions (Next Month's Plan)

_____
_____
_____

In 1607, Cervantes, a Spanish novelist, poet, painter, and play-wright, said, "Tell me the company you keep, and I'll tell you who you are." His comments hold true today. Leaders with resilient networks outperform their peers. The main reason for this result is the types of internal and external networks with which Champions associate. These networks provide:

- Useful perspectives on knowing what is current and what is on the horizon.

- Ideas for new learning and development, which in turn can improve performance for themselves and the organization.

According to a 2002 *Harvard Business Review* article titled "Seven Principles for Cultivating Communities of Practice," written by Wenger, McDermott, and Snyder, there are seven principles to re-member when building communities of practice.

1. **Design is organic.** The purpose of a design is not to impose a structure but to help the community develop. Which community design elements are most appropriate depends on the community's stage of development, its environment, member cohesiveness, and the kinds of knowledge it shares.

2. **Bring in outside perspectives.** The design brings into the dia-logue information from outside the community about what the community could achieve.

3. **Accept everyone.** The architecture invites different levels of participation and different types of involvement, which could in-clude bringing in the interests and expertise of staff, customers, and suppliers. The interactions might be semiprivate or private, or take place at a community event.

4. **Develop public and private community spaces.** The key to designing community spaces is to orchestrate activities in both public and private spaces that use the strength of individual relationships to enrich events and to use events to strengthen individual relationships.

5. **Focus on the community's value.** Value is key to community life, because participation in most communities is voluntary. The value of the exchanges that occur within the communities of practice might not be evident immediately. Therefore it is key to focus on the value of the community throughout its lifetime.

6. **Design for safe interaction.** Communities of practice are neutral places, separate from the everyday work pressures of people's jobs. They are places where people feel the freedom to ask for candid advice, share their opinions, and try out their wild ideas without repercussions. They are places that people can drop by to hear about the latest tool, exchange industry gossip, or chat about technical issues without fear of committing to action plans.

7. **Balance large and small community needs.** A mix of idea-sharing forums and tool-building projects fosters casual connections as well as directed community action. Regular meetings, teleconferences, website activity, and informal lunches help create the pulse of the community.(retrieved September 17 2001 from http://hbswk.hbs.edu/archive/2855.html)

Champions drive results through their relationships, innovation, and knowledge. Communities of practice are voluntary; success over time stems from their ability to sufficiently generate enough excitement, relevance, and value to attract and engage members and, in some cases, future employees for the organization. In an era in which existing and prospective customers are expecting rapid and accurate answers to questions, designing an organization that uses its internal and external network will play an important role in quickly transferring the knowledge necessary to address customers' issues.

AGILE ILLUSTRATION

One company we have worked with in the Asia Pacific region is Aedas Limited. Aedas has become a successful architectural firm because their executives constantly develop themselves as Agile Business Leaders. Aedas is a multidisciplinary group that does architecture, interiors, urban design and landscape, and property consultancy. They employ approximately twenty-six hundred people throughout the United Kingdom, Asia, Central and Eastern Europe, the Middle East, and North and South America. Aedas thus has an opportunity for building diverse internal and external networks. Achieving its level of success has hinged on the basic notion of hiring highly qualified and experienced staff from diverse backgrounds and cultures and using the strength of its network. Aedas incorporates this thinking with its core value of "excellent design."

Keith Griffiths, chairman of Aedas, understands the importance of building his internal and external network. He knows that the ability to rapidly identify and locate individuals with particular knowledge is a significant source of competitive differentiation in the marketplace. Keith has close connections with the University

Of Hong Kong (HKU) and the Chinese University. He is an honorary professor of architecture at HKU. Several staff members from Aedas have given lectures at both universities. This relationship not only gives Aedas access to the top students before they graduate, but it also helps stimulate the designer's creativity with new ideas. Aedas's leaders engage with their internal and external network to rapidly identify individuals who have subject-matter expertise or existing knowledge assets, in order to provide the best answer to a client problem. They use their communities of practice as a forum for individuals to share a variety of perspectives around a common topic and create a breeding ground for innovation. As organizations grow in size, geographical scope, and complexity, it is increasingly apparent that sponsoring and supporting communities of practice, as Aedas does, can improve organizational performance.

THEORY IN PRACTICE ACTIVITY 3.3

CHECKING THE AVAILABILITY
OF YOUR NETWORK

Objective of this exercise: To examine the accessibility and availability of your internal and external networks to help deal effectively with the complex and challenging situations that arise in your role as a leader.

Instructions:

1. Review the definitions below for Your Personal Network.
2. Write the names of people you know who fit the appropriate description in the circles on the Your Personal Network diagram.

   a. People you know fit into more than one cate-gory, put them in as many times as they qualify.
   b. If you can't think of someone for a particular circle, leave it blank.
   c. If you think *you* are the best match for that circle, write your name.

Your Personal Network

Definitions

Mentors (*people used for direction*): Mentors help with clarity and are essential when you are confused about the future. Their wealth of experiential or professional knowledge is there for you to observe and emulate. They are people with whom you can brainstorm about accomplishing your goals. They are good benchmarks.

Supporters (*people used for relief*): Supporters are the people you can depend on in a crisis. There is no end to their willingness to help "anytime." They can deal with any challenge and offer all kinds of assistance. A supporter is someone you can call at 3 a.m.

Contenders (*people used for opposition*): Contenders disagree and challenge your thinking to help you out of the tunnel-vision rut. They energize and promote clear thinking by continually asking you to justify your thoughts and opinions.

Connectors (*people used for linkups*): Connectors can guide you in the right direction. They know the people to contact and the places to locate products or services to help you accomplish your task.

Motivators (*people used for energizing*): Motivators are people who can shed a positive light on your situation and keep your hopes and interests high. You can count on them to see the silver lining in the clouds. These people give the task the energy it needs to keep going.

Partners (*people used for task accomplishment*): Partners are subject matter experts who accomplish tasks because of their knowledge, wisdom, information, thinking styles, approaches, and values. Partners help to ensure that all valuable information has been gathered.

YOUR PERSONAL NETWORK ASSESSMENT

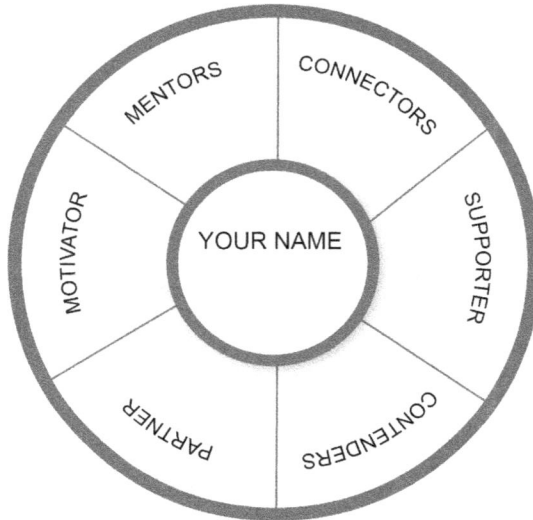

MENTORS	observe, emulate and share experience and knowledge
SUPPORTER	can be depended on in a crisis; they will help whenever you need them
CONTENDER	challenge your thinking and cause you to focus more clearly on issues
CONNECTORS	link you to people, places, things & ideas
MOTIVATORS	share similar interests and celebrate your successes
SME	have the knowledge, wisdom and information needed to deliver an outcome

YOUR PERSONAL NETWORK—PERSONAL ANALYSIS QUESTIONS

After entering the people in your internal and external network into the circles, ask yourself the following questions to analyze the accessibility and availability of your external and internal network.

1. *Do I have all my circles filled in?* If you don't, what area of 'Your Personal Network' are weak and may reduce your opportunities to be effective?

2. *Are all the circles filled in with people to whom I have access?* If so, how might this cause a breakdown in communication or make using the resources of this person more difficult?

3. *Do I have different people's names in each category, or am I the only one in my personal network?* The statement "no man is an island" is very relevant here. We all need a diverse group of people around us.

4. *Does one person's name appear in all the circles?* Am I overburdening the only person in my personal network and potentially causing our relationship to burn out? Also, if that one person leaves my network, for whatever reason, who am I left with in my network?

The ability to locate, access, and apply existing intellectual capital to new situations is an important element of success for the Champion. An enormous benefit and importance accrue in encouraging all employees across an organization to freely share their ideas by building and using a network to help tap into the collective knowledge of the organization and the broader knowledge outside the organization. Champions create methods for harnessing and managing the organization's collective knowledge and wisdom, and as a result, continually develop themselves as better leaders.

6

CHAMPION TRAIT #2

▲ Responsive ▼

It's not the strongest species that survive, nor the most intelligent, but the ones most responsive to change.

CHARLES DARWIN

With competitive pressures limiting a company's ability to raise prices, responsiveness is one of the few remaining business growth sources. Being responsive brings a kind of speed and agility to an organization that can be leveraged into an even greater competitive advantage. Responsiveness involves being decisive and having the ability to make and to act on difficult decisions swiftly and well. It also means acknowledging and understanding the needs and priorities of another person, whether a client, a vendor, or someone working within the organization. Champions are willing to respond to the situation and use their talents in the best possible way. They are prepared for uncertainty and unplanned events because they know the reality of the current on-demand business and operating environment.

A Champion's response to demands depends greatly on the Champion's attitude, stamina, and desire for ongoing learning. Champions have the ability to focus and to share knowledge and ideas in order to improve processes and products—the characteristics that make a Champion responsive. In some cases, responding to demand means you have a different opinion today than you did yesterday. However, this could also be perceived negatively as being wishy-washy or too political. We contend, rather, that it relates to adaptable thinking and is used as a means of striving to constantly stay abreast of people's changing needs and situations by being flexible, fluid, and free. Leaders should let people know why their position is different at any point in time than it was before the triggering event.

AGILE ILLUSTRATION

Mohandas Gandhi regularly changed his mind—often publicly. An aide once asked him how he could so freely contradict this week what he had said just last week. The great man replied, "Because this week I know better." Responsive leaders are willing to adapt and evolve into situations by changing their position and their way of doing things.

Responsive leaders are able to identify the explicit and implicit needs of the people they interact with and use the understanding of those needs to try and fulfill them, whenever required. Champions are generally interested in and concerned about the well-being of their people. They are more than willing to work together and less likely to be callous or indifferent. Champions have the ability to identify needs and priorities and to act upon them in a direct and consistent manner. They are always ready to accept responsibility. As a result, they are respected, trusted, and perceived as reliable and useful to the organization.

In this on-demand global environment, responsiveness to customers' unique and changing needs has become an issue of customer demand, global supply, talent, and flexibility'. The explanations below expand on these four areas.

1. *Responding to customer's demands.* Understanding the customer's inventory levels, ordering patterns, path to profitability, and unique business challenges allows Champions to serve their customers better. If you really listen to your customer, you will know exactly what your customer is saying, and you will be able to better explain how your product or service is of value. Quickness in anticipating and responding to customer demands is an important ingredient of competitive advantage. Customer-centric strategies keep the business focused on big-picture goals that can truly build value for your organization.

2. *Identify global supply.* Champions have the optimal mix of local and overseas suppliers and can respond better to the fluctuations in their business. Understanding which are the right suppliers helps with sourcing materials to keep the costs down, reducing long lead times and allowing the project to change at a moment's notice as the situation requires.

3. *Maximize use of talent.* Champions know that success lies in the ability to build respect and trust among the people with whom they

interact. When people can communicate well, regardless of geographic boundaries, leaders can begin to help increase productivity and responsiveness. Champions must give their team members quick access to whatever resources are currently available. When geographically dispersed staff need to collaborate, Champions respond by taking advantage of communication tools such as e-meetings, virtual whiteboards, and portals. Champions possess analytical, emotional, and communication skills to ensure that they are able to respond positively, effectively, and with agility.

4. *Provide business flexibility.* You can't be responsive to customer needs with a one-size-fits-all strategy. The ability to reconfigure business processes quickly and accurately, produce quality work, and meet deadlines is important in a world of unprecedented business and market pressures. To meet business needs and on-demand requirements, Champions integrate open, efficient, customer-centric infrastructures.

THEORY IN PRACTICE ACTIVITY 3.4

CIRCLES OF RESPONSIVENESS

Objective of this exercise: To help you examine your attitudes toward the areas and activities in your life as a leader and the control you feel you have in relation to those areas of leadership.

Instructions: Follow the following steps.

Step 1. Make a list of what your energy and attention have been focused on in your role as a leader; in other words, what is your to-'do list' for this week? Include areas such as concerns, conversations, performance objectives, requirements, expectations, and so on.

Step 2. Using the "Circles of Responsiveness Frame of Mind" graphic following, categorize each of the items in your list to correspond with the appropriate Circle of Responsiveness.

For example, if your list consisted of seven items you might divide your list as follows.

Lead project meeting   *I Can Influence*
Meeting with key client   *Luck of the Draw*

Deal with problem employee   *Luck of the Draw*

Discuss new strategy with boss   *I Can Control*

Complete budget forms   *I Can Control*

Write proposal for new client   *I Can Influence*

Develop program for new employee   *I Can Influence*

Circles of Responsiveness Frame of Mind

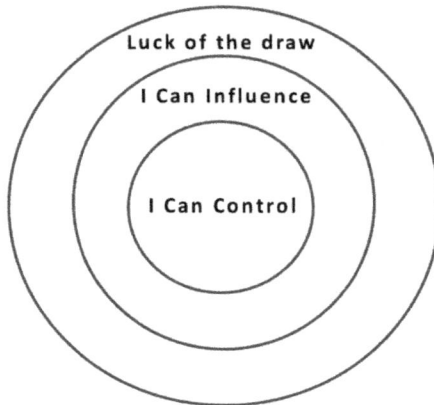

Circles of Responsiveness Frame of Mind Definitions

Luck of the Draw

- The world around me is unpredictable.

- Results, for me, are contingent on other forces—for example, luck, chance, or other unforeseen factors.

- When I think about factors in this circle I think about their deficiencies.

- Components in this circle affect my life by consistently making me feel underloaded or overloaded.

- I have little energy to deal with the task at hand, knowing that the areas I am concerned with fall into this area.

I Can Influence

- The world around me is a product of the things that I can influence.

- Results, for me, are contingent on my belief that I understand the problem, and I have the resources to cope with the issue successfully.

- When considering factors in this circle I think I have a fundamental conviction that these situations will make sense in the end, even though I may undergo great difficulties, challenges, and complexities along the way,

- Components in this circle affect my life by consistently making me aware of my purpose and what I can influence.

- Effort (time and energy) is needed to resolve the issues in this circle.

Step 3. After reviewing your results, ask yourself the following questions:

- How are my action items distributed across the Circles of Responsiveness?

- What do I notice happens when a lot of my time and energy is spent dealing with actions that consistently fall in the "Luck of the Draw" circle?

- How do I feel when I focus on the activities within my control or in the "I Can Control" circle?

- What actions can I create or develop in the "I Can Control" circle that would potentially impact the "I Can Influence" circle?

- How can I move my energy and efforts from the "Luck of the Draw" circle toward the "I Can Control" circle?

Responsiveness Challenge

Time is a luxury most leaders don't have. As the pace of business increases, responsiveness becomes one of the key determinants of success. The challenge with this Theory in Practice Activity is for you to decide how you can stay focused on the "I Can Control" circle. It will also be important for you to decide how you can move the actions that are currently in your "Luck of the Draw" circle toward the "I Can Influence" circle or the "I Can Control" circle. If a leader spends too much time on "Luck of the Draw," he can become less focused, less motivated, and less productive. We challenge you to observe and understand how you interpret the control you have over your actions. The "I Can Control" circle encourages you to be aware of yourself and your abilities. The "Luck of the Draw" circle suggests that any action is out of your control and perhaps not within the realm of achieving success.

7

CHAMPION COMPETENCY #3

▲ Understand Self and Use Strengths ▼

Champions recognize their talents and know how to fully deploy their strengths and compensate for their weaknesses. They recognize and manage their emotions and know what type of effect they have on themselves and others. Champions know how to use their personal strengths to motivate themselves and others toward action. They are conscious of their core beliefs and redirect destructive behaviors and barriers to performance so that continuous improvements can be made. Champions celebrate and respect achievements, and in full awareness of their own strengths and limitations, direct their attention to building the strengths of others as well as organizations.

AGILE ANALOGY

Someone once said to Eileen, "Eileen, while you came from very humble beginnings, you have been passionate about being a good mother to your three children, you've been married for over thirty years, you've hosted and produced a radio show and a TV show, you worked hard to get your Ph.D. In two-and-a-half years, you won numerous awards, you wrote a couple of books, and you are sought after around the world as a speaker, educator, and facilitator. You're a Champion, so how do you do it?" Eileen's response was as follows:

I was actually surprised by the question, because I never really thought of myself as a Champion or for that matter, about all the things I had done. I was surprised because I didn't consciously set out to be a Champion. I did set out to use all of the talents and strengths I had to improve the conditions around me. Then I realized perhaps this was part of the answer. Being a Champion is part of who you are and how you work with people and use your talents. It is a leader's unique character that attribute to his or her thoughts and actions.

In order to achieve what I had done, I had to become very clear about what was important to me. I had to decide if I wanted to focus and use my abilities for building relationships, making money, supporting a belief or driving myself to my personal standard, or not. It also meant, at some level, I had to become very clear about how I wanted to impact the people in my life and whom I worked with. It also meant I had to become very clear about what old teachings from the past no longer worked for me in the present, or for that matter, never worked for me in the past! I had to be open, receptive, and humble to improving, supporting, engaging, and achieving. I had to be willing to take risks, trust myself that I could do it, and associate with people who could help me when I needed it and help them when it contributed to the bigger picture.

I had to determine who I wanted to be in this life and then live it. I had to know and accept that the way to get where I'm going might change, but the principles by which I live do not. I had to understand myself and use my strengths to make things happen.

When we include this competency of "understanding self and using strengths," we are really talking about Champions having self-awareness. Leaders who have a high degree of self-awareness recognize how their feelings affect them, other people, and their job performance. Self-aware leaders know that if tight deadlines bring out the worst in them, they need to plan time carefully and get work done well in advance. Other leaders with high self-awareness will understand their clients' impact on their mood and have better insight into their own frustrations. We are not talking about leaders with such strong self-awareness that they are overly critical or unrealistically hopeful. Instead, we are speaking about leaders who are cognizant of their emotions, strengths, weaknesses, needs, and drives, and who use them for achieving what they want. They are leaders who are comfortable in their own skin. In many cases these are the leaders who, when it comes to using their strengths, build a bridge and get over it!

AGILE ANALOGY

One of the simplest tools for gaining self-awareness has been the presence of a mirror. Written records about the use of man-made mirrors date back as far as 1500 BC. Considering your "reflected image" has long been considered by philosophers to be a stimulus to self-focus and self-awareness, because perception of yourself and your immediate situation affects how you behave, what you believe, and how you feel.

Some interesting studies have been conducted in regard to self-awareness and mirrors. In one study, researchers found that participants used an increased number of first-person pronouns when they looked in a mirror to answer questions. Trick-or-treaters on Halloween were less likely to "steal" extra candy if a mirror was placed at the door of the home. People who stuttered increased their "verbal disfluencies" when they looked at themselves in a mirror. Researchers found that individuals who use a mask cloak themselves in anonymity and conceal their identity, leading to de-individuation. This ABL competency encourages Agile Business Leaders to physically and metaphorically look in the mirror and become more aware of whom they are and the role they play in the context of the organization. They must be honest with themselves and others. They must be authentic.

Authenticity refers to a link between the inner and the outer person. It goes beyond telling the truth; authenticity demonstrates a total congruence between who you are and what you do and say. Truly authentic leaders are open both to their gifts and to their underdeveloped qualities. They understand that they have an influential voice and can make a more profound contribution to the organization.

In all of our research and experience, working with leaders and having conversations with those leading and those being led, we have identified eight values that continue to surface every time we investigate solid leaders. These eight basic values consistently govern a successful leader's character. They are integrity, honesty, building and maintaining good relationships, keeping commitments, trustworthiness, being there for one's family and for others, caring, and being ethical. The Champion not only understands personal values and the personal goals he sets for himself, he is also able to speak accurately and openly about where he is headed and why.

Champions do not just identify personal values; they also examine how their behaviors support their values. Saying you value honesty is one thing. It is another matter to take a stand in the midst of a business decision that would benefit you if you were dishonest. If a Champion says she values honesty, then she will define specific behaviors that demonstrate that value. Champions perceive themselves as capable of behaving appropriately and seeing those behaviors as being appropriate to the situation before they ever engage in them. The leader in the role of Champion presents as a wise sage with a strong foundation of values.

Some leaders we talked to while developing this chapter made comments that concerned us. For that reason we are going to leave each person's name off of the following quotes. When we asked these leaders about their strengths and how they might improve, this is what they said:

- People tell me I can't communicate with my staff. But I don't have a problem communicating with people; it's just that people have a problem communicating with me.

- One of my best strengths is to do the "Scorpion Dance" with the people who come into my office and challenge my leadership. They come in, and like a scorpion, I sniff them out and decide if we will work together. If I don't think it will work, like a scorpion I make them my dinner.

- I like my job as a leader. It's easy and I don't have to do much. I really don't want to do any more than I have to. The salary I get allows me to keep bowling, and that's all that matters to me. I think bowling is one of the few things I'm good at.

- I want to keep being a processing machine till I leave this job. I keep my head down and do what I have to do. I might have strengths, but I don't want to try anything different. I just want to keep doing what I'm doing and keep out of the drama at work and with my staff.

Leaders act, feel, and perform in accordance with what they imagine to be true about themselves and their environment. Some leaders have a need to emphasize their status as a victim, as a viable way of figuring out who and what they want to be. They do not know who they are because they do not know who they are not. Their perception of the reasons for their success (or failure) determines the amount of effort they expend on an activity. For the leaders reading this book, this result means that what you imagine to be true can in fact become true. We interpret our environment in such a way as to maintain a self-image, whether that image is positive or negative.

- Leaders who are not confident and believe they have few strengths, will

- Shy away from difficult tasks that are viewed as personal threats.

- Have low aspirations and weak commitment to their goals.

- Tend to dwell on personal deficiencies when faced with difficult tasks.

- Slacken their efforts and give up quickly in the face of difficulties.

- Respond slowly to rebuilding confidence following failures or setbacks.

- Fall easy victim to stress and depression, which can negatively impact the immune system.

Leaders who lack self-awareness are prone to make decisions that bring on inner turmoil because they tread on buried values. We believe choosing to not understand yourself is largely a matter of pride.

Understanding and believing in yourself as a leader who has the strengths to positively propel yourself to success can create a strong sense of self-worth, enhance your accomplishments, and improve your personal well-being in many ways. Leaders who understand and value their strengths approach threatening situations with assurance.

- Produce personal accomplishments.

- Choose to perform more challenging tasks.

- Recover more quickly when setbacks occur.

- Lower their vulnerability to depression.

- Set higher goals and have a firmer commitment to them.

- Exert greater effort when they fail to master a challenge.

- Have higher success rates in reducing health-impairing habits.

- Have stronger perseverance, which contributes to performance accomplishments.

Remember that action and self-awareness are not mutually exclusive. Champions who have a realistic positive view about their capabilities to function at a high level of performance determine for themselves how they feel, think, and motivate. Sure, there are times you make mistakes or have those embarrassing moments of making a Freudian click on your computer. The Champion possesses wisdom, which we define as "'acting with knowledge while simultaneously doubting what one knows." The decisions of a self-aware Champion interlock with personal values; consequently, the Champion finds work personally rewarding and energizing.

AGILE ILLUSTRATION

The concept of advocating that a person must understand his strengths dates back as far as 4 BC. An inscription on the entrance to the ancient Temple of Apollo at Delphi reads "Know Thyself." Delphi was a major site for the worship of the god Apollo. It was also home of the sanctuary where every four years athletes from all over the Greek world competed in the Pythian Games, the precursor to the Olympic Games. The concept of being a Champion is synonymous with being an Olympian. Someone who knows those areas well is Dr. LeRoy Walker.

LeRoy is a friend and mentor of Eileen's. He has an enormous amount of experience and talent in assessing and motivating athletes to become champions. He has helped many people over many years increase their performance by understanding themselves and using their strengths.

LeRoy is one of the most successful track and field coaches in the United States. Throughout his career, he was coach at North Carolina Central University, where he helped produce 111 All-Americans, 40 National Champions, and 12 Olympians as part of the U.S. Track and Field Teams competing in France, Italy, Germany, the USSR, and West Africa. He has also coached Olympic teams from Ethiopia, Israel, Jamaica, Kenya, and Trinidad-Tobago. Twenty years after coaching the U.S. Olympic team, he agreed to use his strengths, knowledge, and experience to become president of the U.S. Olympic Committee. He has been the chancellor of North Carolina Central University, worked with the USA/People's Republic of China Athletics group, and served as a member of the All-China Physical Education and Sports Committee.

Bud Greenspan is an eight-time Emmy Award–winning film director, writer, and producer, mostly known for his sports documen-
taries. He is often quoted as saying, "Dr. LeRoy Walker is an icon.
As an athlete, coach, and educator, he has influenced thousands to
not only enter the athletic arena but the arena of life. It has been
written, 'Ask not alone for victory; ask for courage. For, if you can
endure, you bring honor to us all.' Dr. Walker has brought honor to
us all."

We said we believe LeRoy Walker is a Champion. You might
wonder, "Where does it begin for the Champion? How is it that
Champions create other Champions?" The answer might amuse
you. LeRoy became a sports champion because of a dare. As a kid
in high school he did not play football in any capacity, but during
his third year of college, he tried out for the football team because
a friend dared him. As a college student he only weighed 155
pounds (small for a football player). He was so small, he could not
even fill out his uniform and equipment, and the trainer had to alter
his shoulder pads. On the day of the tryouts, the coach convinced
him he had natural talents and should be the backup quarterback
for the team. LeRoy discovered he could pass, kick, and run. Running was his biggest asset if he ever got away from the defense.
The opportunity to play quarterback came one day; LeRoy eventually went on to lead Benedict College to the conference championship that year and was named a football All-American by the *Pitts-
burgh Courier*, the first such honor bestowed on a Benedict player.

LeRoy, a natural athlete and coach, works with other athletes to
create champions. His goal is to make sure they feel personally
connected to their cause and that they take ownership in their performance program. He wants his athletes to understand themselves
and use their strengths to achieve.

It might not come as a surprise that LeRoy's values, character, and behavior are aligned to the International Olympic Charter (the fundamental principles are the essential values of "Olympism"). The first fundamental principle in the Charter reads,

> *Olympism is a philosophy of life, exalting and combining (in a balanced whole) the qualities of body, will and mind. By blending sport with culture and education, Olympism seeks to create a way of life based on the joy of effort, the educational value of good example and respect for universal fundamental ethical principles.*

(Retrieved September 20, 2011, https://sites.google.com/a/olympismproject.org/olympism-project/)

It is no wonder that LeRoy Walker was inducted into the U.S. Olympic Athlete Hall of Fame; was recognized by the city of Atlanta, which declared June 11 as LeRoy Walker Day; and received the highest honor by the International Olympic Committee, the Olympic Order. All of LeRoy's achievements can be credited to his ability of playing to his strengths and setting an example for others to do the same. He is, without a doubt, a Champion and someone from whom Eileen has learned a great deal. LeRoy will be quick to tell you, "Stay focused, play to your strengths, consider what others have to say, challenge your thinking, and be willing to do better."

If you think you are too small as a leader to make a difference, then you have never been in a tent with a mosquito! Champions know what they are passionate about and have the courage to go out and do it.

We close this section with the words and desires of the Cowardly Lion and the Tin Man in *The Wizard of Oz*. They seem to sum up nicely the concepts of a leader needing to understand self and use strengths. Clearly a leader with traits of the Champion will not need to visit the Wizard anytime soon, because he definitely has 'nerve' and a 'heart'!

Lyrics from "If I Only Had a Brain"

Tin Man: When a man's an empty kettle

He should be on his mettle

And yet I'm torn apart

Just because I'm presumin'

That I could be a human

If I only had a heart

I'd be tender, I'd be gentle

And awful sentimental

Regarding love and art

I'd be friends with the sparrows

And the boy that shoots the arrows

If I only had a heart

(Note: The word "mettle" in these lyrics means vigor and strength of spirit or temperament, staying quality, stamina, quality of temperament, or disposition, as in: A leader with mettle is destined to be successful.)

THEORY IN PRACTICE ACTIVITY 3.5

THE FOUR PARTS OF YOU

Ancient Roman philosophers often referred to and praised the Roman virtues as the qualities of life to which every Roman citizen should aspire and the ideal they envisioned for their republic. Roman virtues represented what the Roman people wanted to be, and what they admired in their heroes. Roman virtues are also the traits or qualities against which a leader can measure her own behavior and character. The fifteen Roman virtues are as follows:

1. Authority—The sense of one's social standing, built up through experience.

2. Humor—Ease of manner, courtesy, openness, and friendliness.

3. Mercy—Mildness and gentleness.

4. Dignity—A sense of self-worth, personal pride.

5. Tenacity—Strength of mind, the ability to stick to one's purpose.

6. Frugality—Economy and simplicity of style, without being miserly.

7. Gravity—A sense of the importance of the matter at hand, responsibility and earnestness.

8. Respectability—The image that one presents as a respectable member of society.

9. Humanity—Refinement, civilization, learning, and being cultured.

10. Industriousness—Hard work.

11. Dutifulness—More than religious piety; a respect for the natural order socially, politically, and religiously. Includes the ideas of patriotism and devotion to others.

12. Prudence—Foresight, wisdom, and personal discretion.

13. Wholesomeness—Health and cleanliness.

14. Sternness—Seriousness, self-control.

15. Truthfulness—Honesty in dealing with others.

Objective of this exercise: To assess and compare your emotional, mental, physical, and spiritual components against the fifteen Roman virtues, to determine what qualities you would like to keep or to which you aspire.

Instructions:

Step 1: Listed below are four columns that incorporate the four parts of each person: emotional, mental, physical, and spiritual. In each of the columns below, a list of words related to that human factor appear, along with the corresponding Roman virtue. From the list below, circle five words *in each column* that complete the statement, "I am . . ."

The Four Parts of You

Emotional	Mental	Physical	Spiritual
Experiencing the fundamental sensations of the central nervous system through feelings, emotions, and attitudes.	Development of thoughts, ideas, concepts, rational thinking and logic; logic used in understanding and decision-making.	What the body has learned and the skills developed for body existence, movement, and sensations.	Acquiring knowledge created from understanding through experience, senses, perception, and intuition
Affectionate (Mercy)	Alert (Perseverance)	Active (Perseverance)	Authentic (Truthfulness)
Caring (Mercy)	Accepting (Dignity)	Athletic (Industriousness)	Aware (Authority)
Courage (Dutiful)	Wisdom (Prudence)	Fair (Gravity)	Reasonable (Gravity)
Enthusiastic (Humor)	Assertive (Tenacity)	Persistent (Tenacity)	Balanced (Respectable)
Exciting (Humor)	Confident (Dignity)	Brave (Dutiful)	Charismatic (Respectable)
Courageous (Tenacity)	Dignified (Humanity)	Relaxed (Humor)	Centered (Authority)
Fun-loving (Humor)	Creative (Tenacity)	Soft (Mercy)	Devoted (Dutiful)
Exuberant (Humor)	Determined (Tenacity)	Elegant (Respectable)	Inspired (Prudence)
Happy (Humor)	Disciplined (Tenacity)	Energetic (Industriousness)	Fulfilled (Dignity)
Patriotic (Dutiful)	Hopeful (Dutiful)	Graceful (Respectable)	Complete (Authority)
Joyful (Humor)	Learned (Humanity)	Feminine (Dignity)	Imaginative (Prudence)
Important (Authority)	Decisive (Tenacity)	Masculine (Dignity)	Genuine (Truthful)
Open (Truthful)	Accountable (Gravity)	Healthy (Wholesome)	Controlled (Stern)
Positive (Humor)	Cultured (Humanity)	Powerful (Authority)	Diligent (Industrious)
Playful (Humor)	Realistic (Authority)	Strong (Industriousness)	Unique (Dignity)
Tender (Mercy)	Resourceful (Industrious)	Sexy (Dignity)	Whole (Dignity)
		Calm (Dutiful)	Noble (Dignity)
		Lively (Industrious)	

Trusting (Gravity)	Responsible (Frugality)	Dynamic (Humor)	Self-aware (Prudence)
Warm (Mercy)	Successful (Tenacity)	Involved (Industrious)	Perceptive (Prudence)
Responsive (Gravity)	Organized (Prudence)	Functional (Industrious)	Empathic (Humor)
Silly (Humor)		Natural (Wholesome)	Fair (Gravity)
Serious (Stern)	Optimist (Dutiful)	Prepared (Tenacity)	Honest (Truthful)
Spontaneous (Humor)	Effective (Respectable)	Equipped (Tenacity)	Sincere (Truthful)
Courteous (Humor)	Independent (Tenacity)		Articulate (Humanity)
Friendly (Humor)	Direct (Truthful)		
	Intelligent (Prudence)		

Step 2: From the five words you have circled in each column, choose one word in each column and write it on the line below.

_____   _____   _____   _____

Step 3: Insert your four final words written at the bottom of each column into the following sentence,

"I, [your name here], am a

_____, _____, _____, and _____

person."

Step 4: Read the sentence in Step 3 out loud and decide how you feel when you hear the sentence. Consider the following five questions:

1. Does this sentence describe who you believe you are?

2. Does this sentence capture the characteristics or virtues you would like to have as a leader?

3. How would a leader with these characteristics or virtues be perceived in your organization?

4. Would a leader having these characteristics or virtues succeed in the business you are in?

5. Are there other characteristics or virtues you wish were in your sentence in Step 3? If so, how do you plan to make them part of your leadership capabilities and strengths moving forward in your development?

Now is the time for you as a leader to recognize your opportunities in life. Define who you are and how you want to succeed. When a leader learns to live to the highest of his innate abilities, he begins to realize that this shift in direction and perception also begins to positively impact the outcome.

What blocks most leaders from creating their dreams in life is their fear of being who they are. Sometimes this is a fear of non-acceptance from others. Sometimes it is a fear of failing. Sometimes it is simply that the leader's whole life has conditioned him to live in a manner alien to who he really is. When a leader is afraid, he is more likely to miss or neglect opportunities when they appear. When a leader is true to himself and his instincts and potential, fear becomes transformed into successful action.

8

CHAMPION COMPETENCY #4

Champions expect a great deal from themselves and others. They set high goals and work hard to achieve them by staying committed to analyzing the effects of their own and others' actions and by continuously exploring and experimenting with ways to improve products, processes, services, and systems. One military leader we talked to while facilitating his staff retreat said, "I'm in the military, and I have to tell you, we have a strange feeling about the phrase 'we are going to have a retreat.' We don't like 'retreat' in the military." In a sense, like this military leader, Champions also do not like to retreat or give up. Champions are strong individuals who strive to improve or meet high standards of excellence and are not likely to retreat easily (unless there is a need to adapt and appropriately respond). Champions know they will not achieve their goals without hard work and persistence.

Champions set expectations and venture out to develop the business. They show a willingness to take risks, and to be innovative and experiment with different ideas and concepts in order to find new and better ways of doing and achieving. It is not about giving up. It is about realigning thinking. Champions are always in the process of creating or seizing an opportunity and pursuing it regardless of the resources at hand. They approach tasks related to succeeding because they believe success is due to a high level of ability and effort, which they are confident they have. To have this type of personal motivation, the Champion has a considerable amount of self-control. She handles business pressures and sets expectations to achieve. Interruptions in achieving expectations motivate the Champion to work harder next time. Champions are comfortable in stressful situations and are challenged rather than discouraged by setbacks.

Champions know that things do not necessarily happen for the best, but as a leader the Champion is able to make the best of a situation or events. The secret of setting high expectations is constancy of purpose. It has been said that "if a person doesn't know what port they are sailing to, no wind is favorable"; the same is true of setting high expectations. We often tell our clients, "If you don't know where you are going, you will probably end up there."

There is evidence that a leader's personality has a strong impact on setting expectations and achieving them. A summary of different studies we investigated revealed that when leaders have eight specific natural personality traits, they tend to set higher expectations and achieve more. The eight personality traits for setting higher expectations include:

1. Having commitment and determination to achieve their purpose.

2. Able to lead groups well.

3. Obsessed with seizing opportunities.

4. Tolerant of risk, ambiguity, and uncertainty.

5. Innovative in their approach to problem solving.

6. Self-reliant and can "go it alone" if necessary.

7. Able to adapt to situations as they arise.

8. Motivated to excel in delivering on expectations.

Setting expectations is not a solely independent process. How Champions identify which relationships they will develop as part of setting expectations is crucial to the success of each venture; the Champion needs to use these relationships to obtain the information, funds, legitimacy, and help to survive and flourish.

AGILE ANALOGY

Barry enjoys fishing. As any fisherman does, he sets high expectations for his trips. In the following story Barry speaks about the need to assess each situation and respond appropriately.

On a recent fishing trip on Stradbroke Island—off the east coast of my home state, Queensland, Australia—I joined my brother Bill, the best fishing trip organizer of all time, for our annual pilgrimage. This particular beach is totally uninhabited and is a mecca for camping and fishing.

On the second day of the trip, I was fishing in the surf, standing in knee-deep water and enjoying the solitude of the moment. I had set my expectations for a great catch that day. All of a sudden, the others on the beach started screaming and whistling; I knew exactly what was happening. I walked back in the water a few steps and looked around for the action; yep, it was a four-meter-long shark. Sharks are common in these waters and can easily affect the expectations you set for a trip (the metaphor for a leader in an organization was not lost on me).

The shark first emerged directly in front of me, about eight meters away. My first reaction was to gasp at the beauty of this incredible creature. She was playing and rolling in the waves, and enjoying the time to frolic. My second reaction was survival. I pulled in my line (I had set high expectations, but landing a shark on the end of my fishing rod while standing in open waters was not part of that expectation). I didn't feel afraid—well, not until several of my fisherman friends, who had downed several bottles of beer while on the shore, decided it would be a good idea to get into the water and pat the shark. It didn't take long for them to come to their senses and give the shark its space. She soon swam out to sea.

Fishing had been exciting up to that point. Now the problem was that the shark had scared off all the fish and the only thing that remained were the fishermen. My expectations would not be achieved that day, and I would have to wait for another time to get the catch of the day.

The Champion accepts things as they are and does not linger over nonproductive tasks. You may think we are suggesting that the Champion should be passive. Not at all. In accepting reality, the Champion gathers all the relevant information, accepts what is happening, and is willing to change the focus of the expectation when he sees that change will improve the organization's prospects or is needed for survival.

Champions know they must work collaboratively to accomplish the organization's goals, even when there are personality or workplace differences. The Champion is willing, as a result, to help everyone take joint ownership of expectations, group commitments, work activities, schedules, and group accomplishments. Taking a communal approach to setting expectations gives the Champion a multidimensional skill that enables seeing a project to completion or setting an expectation in a larger context, with the aid of the eyes of critical others, including customers, competitors, coworkers, and bosses. This approach also allows the Champion to evaluate the relative importance of various viewpoints and develop realistic (yet high) expectations.

Surrounding all of these dimensions, the Champion can comprehend complex situations, which may include planning, making strategic decisions, and working on multiple business ideas simultaneously. Such activity is possible because a leader is both farsighted and nearsighted. A Champion has 20/20 vision and devotes energy to completing the tasks immediately at hand while maintaining that all-important big-picture perspective.

When setting high expectations, the Champion ensures that the target is worth the effort. The Champion personally identifies with the desired achievements and ensures that they represent her personal interests and values. The Champion sets high expectations and goes above and beyond the accepted job description to escape everyday work routines in order to offer bold and innovative ideas and solutions.

THEORY IN PRACTICE ACTIVITY 3.6

TAKE OFF AND SOAR

Objective of this exercise: Using the analogy of an airplane taking off and cruising through the air, this activity is designed to investigate how a leader uses each of the four ABL roles to take to the skies and achieve success. (Note: This activity does not investigate the best way to land. We want to encourage you to keep flying!)

Instructions: This Theory in Practice requires you to let your mind wander and stretch your imagination into the realm of analogies and possibilities. We encourage you to play with ideas and not be grounded by the thought, *I just don't want to take off!*

The diagram below illustrates the three stages of flight takeoff for this Theory in Practice Activity; Taxi, Climb, and Cruise. Using the following airlines—Specialist Airways, Champion Aviation, Strategist Express, and Enabler AirBus—complete the following steps as they relate to the four roles and traits of the Agile Business Leader. Each step offers 'points for consideration' that a pilot needs to be concerned with during takeoff. These points serve as an analogy for what leaders need to consider as they take off and soar.

THREE STAGES OF FLIGHT:

TAXI, CLIMB AND CRUISE

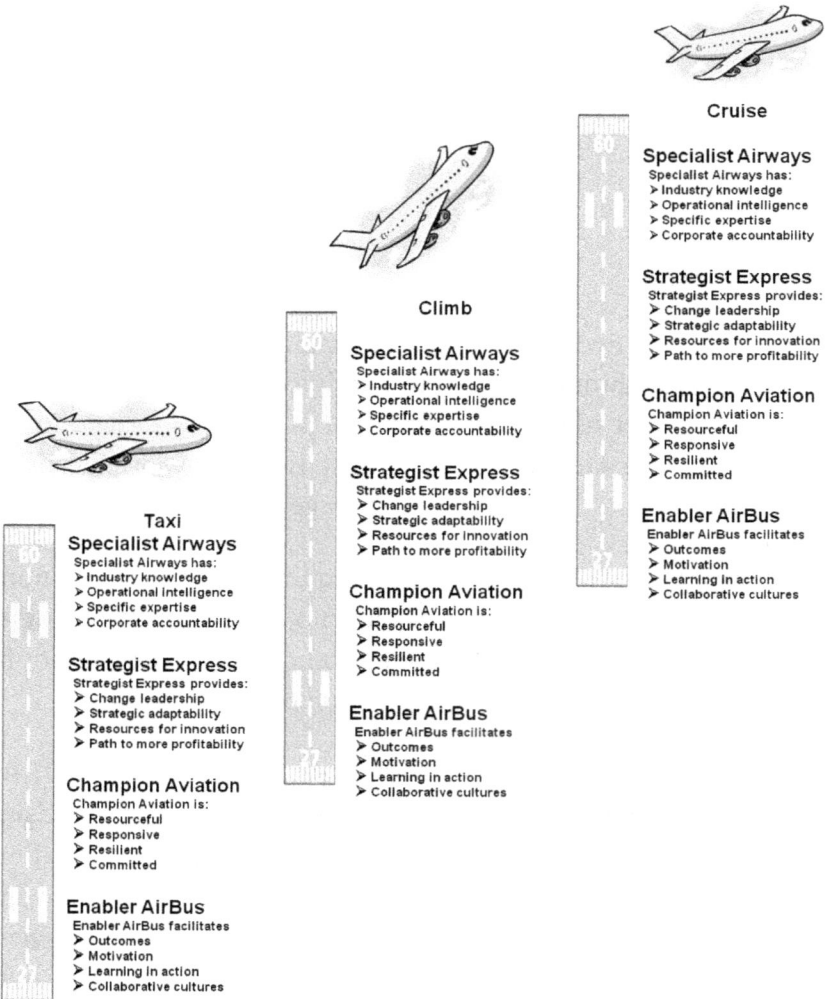

Taxi

Specialist Airways
Specialist Airways has:
➤ Industry knowledge
➤ Operational intelligence
➤ Specific expertise
➤ Corporate accountability

Strategist Express
Strategist Express provides:
➤ Change leadership
➤ Strategic adaptability
➤ Resources for innovation
➤ Path to more profitability

Champion Aviation
Champion Aviation is:
➤ Resourceful
➤ Responsive
➤ Resilient
➤ Committed

Enabler AirBus
Enabler AirBus facilitates
➤ Outcomes
➤ Motivation
➤ Learning in action
➤ Collaborative cultures

Climb

Specialist Airways
Specialist Airways has:
➤ Industry knowledge
➤ Operational intelligence
➤ Specific expertise
➤ Corporate accountability

Strategist Express
Strategist Express provides:
➤ Change leadership
➤ Strategic adaptability
➤ Resources for innovation
➤ Path to more profitability

Champion Aviation
Champion Aviation is:
➤ Resourceful
➤ Responsive
➤ Resilient
➤ Committed

Enabler AirBus
Enabler AirBus facilitates
➤ Outcomes
➤ Motivation
➤ Learning in action
➤ Collaborative cultures

Cruise

Specialist Airways
Specialist Airways has:
➤ Industry knowledge
➤ Operational intelligence
➤ Specific expertise
➤ Corporate accountability

Strategist Express
Strategist Express provides:
➤ Change leadership
➤ Strategic adaptability
➤ Resources for innovation
➤ Path to more profitability

Champion Aviation
Champion Aviation is:
➤ Resourceful
➤ Responsive
➤ Resilient
➤ Committed

Enabler AirBus
Enabler AirBus facilitates
➤ Outcomes
➤ Motivation
➤ Learning in action
➤ Collaborative cultures

Step 1: Taxiing

Review the Points for Consideration needed for this phase of takeoff and answer the following questions as they relate to the ABL roles and traits.

Points for Consideration

• Prior to taxiing, select flight plan in accordance with ability.

• Make sure you have the necessary clearance to proceed.

• Determine speed. *Note:* Long taxi distance can cause heat to collect in tires.

• Understand your taxi turning radius.

• Turn slowly to prevent tire skids.

• Complete taxi in a straight line.

• Exit the runway.

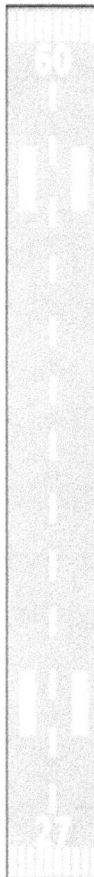

Taxi
Specialist Airways
Specialist Airways has:
➢ Industry knowledge
➢ Operational intelligence
➢ Specific expertise
➢ Corporate accountability

Strategist Express
Strategist Express provides:
➢ Change leadership
➢ Strategic adaptability
➢ Resources for innovation
➢ Path to more profitability

Champion Aviation
Champion Aviation is:
➢ Resourceful
➢ Responsive
➢ Resilient
➢ Committed

Enabler AirBus
Enabler AirBus facilitates:
➢ Outcomes
➢ Motivation
➢ Learning in action
➢ Collaborative cultures

Climb

 Specialist Airways has:

➢ *Industry Knowledge*

1. Which strengths from my knowledge of the industry can I use to help the organization taxi down the runway?

_____

2. What additional industry knowledge do I need in order to exit the runway?

_____

➢ *Operational Intelligence*

1. What flight plan can be developed from the operational intelligence I possess?

_____

2. Do I understand the radius I can work within?

_____

➢ *Specific Expertise*

1. Which expertise can I make available to the group and organization to taxi down the runway?

_____

2. What additional specific expertise do I need in order to exit the runway?

_____

➤ *Corporate Accountability*

1. How do the existing processes for corporate accountability help the organization move down the path of profitability, sustainability, and success?

2. What additional corporate accountability processes could help the organization move through the requirements necessary for 'takeoff'?

Cruise

 Specialist Airways has:

➤ *Industry Knowledge*

1. Which strengths from my knowledge of the industry can I use to help the organization taxi down the runway?

2. What additional industry knowledge do I need in order to exit the runway?

➤ *Operational Intelligence*

1. What flight plan can be developed from the operational intelligence I possess?

2. Do I understand the radius I can work within?

➢ *Specific Expertise*

1. Which expertise can I make available to the group and organization to taxi down the runway?

_____

2. What additional specific expertise do I need in order to exit the runway?

_____

➢ *Corporate Accountability*

1. How do the existing processes for corporate accountability help the organization move down the path of profitability, sustainability, and success?

_____

2. What additional corporate accountability processes could help the organization move through the requirements necessary for 'takeoff'?

_____

Strategist Express provides:

➢ *Change Leadership*

1. What changes would help the organization taxi correctly the runway?

_____

2. What level of speed would be best to initiate a strategy?

_____

➢ *Strategic Adaptability*

1. What must we adapt for the organization to taxi correctly the runway?

_____

2. What must we adapt within the group and organization to be prepared for helping the group and organization take off and soar?

_____

➢ *Resources for Innovation*

1. What resources does the organization have available to start taxiing and maneuvering down the runway?

_____

2. What innovative expertise can we draw on for creating the flight plan to begin the taxiing process?

_____

➢ *Path to More Profitability*

1. What clearance is needed for the taxiing process?

_____

2. What speed is required to begin seeing a profit and avoid skid marks?

_____

Champion Aviation is:

➢ *Resourceful*

1. Which strengths do I have as a resourceful leader as I am taxiing down a runway?

_____

2. In what more efficient way could the organization move forward?

_____

➢ *Responsive*

1. What ways are we being responsive to our customers' needs as they begin to use our products and services?

_____

2. How is the organization's speed of responsiveness allowing us to take flight and avoid skid marks?

_____

➢ *Resilient*

1. How has the organization rebounded from previous flight delays?

_____

2. What are the organization's greatest strength and ability for being able to take off?

_____

➢ *Committed*

1. In what ways does the organization show it is committed to takeoff?

_____

2. Who in the organization is willing to exit the runway and climb to the next height in the industry?

_____

Enabler AirBus facilitates

➢ *Outcomes*

1. What are the immediate outcomes needed to be focused on so the organization can take off?

_____

2. What is the most appropriate speed to achieve our outcomes efficiently?

_____

➢ *Motivation*

1. Which strengths do I have for motivating employees to continue down the runway?

_____

2. What flight plan do I need to focus on to continue to motivate employees with?

_____

➤ *Learning in Action*

1. How can we apply previous taxiing experience to do better on our next flight?

_____

2. How are we communicating what radius we are working with so that we do not bump into other things and damage the organization?

_____

➤ *Collaborative Cultures*

1. What type of collaborative culture do we want to establish for taxiing?

_____

2. What will be the best way to build a collaborative culture to efficiently help the group or organization climb and soar?

_____

Step 2: Climbing

Review the Points for Consideration for this phase of takeoff and answer the following questions as they relate to the ABL roles and traits.

Points for Consideration

- Hold nose of plane in position until positive rate of climb is confirmed.
- Set initial speed.
- Set highest setting.
- Accelerate.
- Set speed to final cruise.

Specialist Airways has:

➢   *Industry Knowledge*

1. Which strengths from my knowledge of the industry can I use to help the organization climb to the height at which we want to operate?

_____

2. What additional industry knowledge do I need in order to exit the runway?

_____

➢   *Operational Intelligence*

1. What flight plan can be developed from the operational intelligence I possess?

_____

2. Do I understand the radius I can work within?

_____

➢   *Specific Expertise*

1. Which expertise can I make available to the group and organization to climb to the altitude we want to achieve?

_____

2. How can I better understand the organization's and the customer's needs to continue to climb to profitability and success?

_____

➢   *Corporate Accountability*

1. How do the existing processes for corporate accountability help the organization accelerate toward profitability, sustainability, and success?

_____

2. What additional corporate accountability process could be added to help the organization climb toward success?

Strategist Express provides:

➢ *Change Leadership*

1. What current conditions make it difficult to hold the organization in position and might cause us to change our heading and course?

---

2. What level of speed would be best to initiate a strategy?

➢ *Strategic Adaptability*

1. What must we adapt within the group and organization to be prepared for any changes in speed or needs for acceleration?

---

2. How would I know we are adapting to the needs of conditions in the industry and organization and, at the same time, staying on course with our strategy?

➢ *Resources for Innovation*

1. What resources does the organization have available to help with acceleration?

---

2. What innovative approach will help us with acceleration and organizational success?

➢ *Path to More Profitability*

1. At what final speed do we as an organization want to be cruising?

_____

2. What direction or position do we need to stay at to help this organization climb?

_____

Champion Aviation is:

➢ *Resourceful*

1. What strengths do I have as a resourceful leader to help the organization continue to climb in order to reach our final cruising speed?

_____

2. What more efficient ways could the organization use to climb toward profitability, sustainability, and success?

_____

➢ *Responsive*

1. During acceleration, what areas within the organization need my greatest attention?

_____

2. How has my speed of responsiveness allowed my group or organization to continue to climb?

_____

➢ *Resilient*

1. How have I continued to determine the rate the organization and customer wants to use in order to climb to profitability and success?

_____

2. What are the greatest strengths and abilities I use to accelerate the organization forward?

_____

➤ *Committed*

1. In what ways do I show I am committed to accelerating within the organization and the industry?

_____

2. What level of commitment do I want to set as my 'cruising speed'?

_____

Enabler AirBus facilitates

➤ *Outcomes*

1. What are the immediate outcomes we will achieve if we accelerate toward a certain height?

_____

2. What is the most appropriate speed to achieve our outcomes efficiently?

_____

➤ *Motivation*

1. Which strengths do I have for motivating employees to climb to greater heights?

_____

2. What is the highest speed toward which I can accelerate my team and organization?

_____

➢ *Learning in Action*

1. How can we take our previous climbing experience and learn to do better on our next flight?

    _____

2. How are we ensuring that the speed we are using to keep the group and organization operational is achieving the heights we are striving toward?

    _____

➢ *Collaborative Cultures*

1. What type of collaborative culture do we want to establish for climbing and reaching new heights?

    _____

2. What is the best way to build a collaborative culture to efficiently help the group or organization climb and soar?

    _____

Step 3: Cruising

Points for Consideration

• Determine what altitude leads to lowest drag.

• Set cruise altitude and level off.

• Determine maximum specific range throughout the flight (i.e., normal or long-range cruise).

• Determine speed.

• Decide if you want to operate on cruise control.

• Decide if you must reduce cruise speed because of head winds.

Specialist Airways has:

➢ *Industry Knowledge*

1. Which strengths from my knowledge of the industry can I use to help the organization cruise to profitability and sustainability?

_____

2. What additional knowledge will help set a cruising altitude for the team and organization?

_____

➢ *Operational Intelligence*

1. What range (long or short range) do I want to use as I help the group and organization cruise?

_____

2. Do I understand the costs and benefits of the group or organization choosing to cruise at this point in time?

_____

➢ *Specific Expertise*

1. Which expertise can I make available to the group and organization to help maintain an altitude with the lowest amount of resistance or drag?

_____

2. What additional expertise do I need to gain to help manage head-winds and reduce the drag on the organization?

_____

➢ *Corporate Accountability*

1. How do the existing processes for corporate accountability help us keep the organization on track?

_____

2. What additional corporate accountability processes could help the organization comfortably maintain its cruising speed?

Strategist Express provides:

➢ *Change Leadership*

1. What changes would help the organization maintain balance and speed?

---

2. What level of speed would be best to initiate a strategy and result in the least amount of resistance and drag?

➢ *Strategic Adaptability*

1. What must we adapt within the group and organization to be prepared for any unforeseen headwinds or changes in industry climate?

---

2. How would I know that we are adapting and at the same time on course with our strategy?

➢ *Resources for Innovation*

1. What resources does the organization or group have available to help it determine what speed or level it wants to operate at in order to maintain a steady course?

---

2. What innovative approaches will help customers, investors, and employees decide that we are the organization of choice and the one they should trust to take their next trip?

➤ *Path to More Profitability*

1. What is the final altitude at which we want to continue to operate?

    _____

2. What headwinds and conditions do we need to be aware of as we travel through the industry?

    _____

Champion Aviation is:

➤ *Resourceful*

1. Which strengths do I have as a resourceful leader to help the organization manage headwinds and travel safely?

    _____

2. What more efficient ways could the organization cruise toward profitability, sustainability, and success?

    _____

➤ *Responsive*

1. While enjoying the comforts of success, what areas within my group and organization need my greatest attention?

    _____

2. How has my speed of responsiveness allowed my group or organization to continue cruising?

    _____

➤ *Resilient*

1. How can I assess that our cruising rate will achieve profitability and success?

    _____

2. What are the greatest strengths and abilities I use for staying on
    course and providing excellent customer service?

    _____

➤ *Committed*

1. In what ways do I show I am committed to staying on board and
    achieving the best outcomes possible?

    _____

2. Who in the organization is willing to exit the runway and climb to
    the next height?

    _____

Enabler AirBus facilitates

➤ *Outcomes*

1. What outcomes will result when our team and organization have
    reached our cruising altitude?

    _____

2. How will we know we are on a descent and will need to react appro-
    priately?

    _____

➤ *Motivation*

1. Which strengths do I have for motivating employees to continue to
    stay on course?

    _____

2. How can I motivate myself and my group to continue to strive for
    excellence while we are cruising?

    _____

➤ *Learning in Action*

1. What can we learn from completing launches to help improve our products and services in the future?

    _____

2. How are we ensuring that our cruising speed will keep the group and organization operational while allowing for a change of course if necessary?

    _____

➤ *Collaborative Cultures*

1. When experiencing a headwind or a bumpy ride, what resources can we use to help foster communication for building a stronger collaborative culture?

    _____

2. How can we take this time to strengthen trust within the group and organization?

    _____

3. What will be the best way to build a collaborative culture to efficiently help the group or organization climb and soar?

    _____

9

CHAMPION TRAIT #3

▲ Resilient ▼

"The reasonable man adapts himself to the world; the unreasonable one persists in trying to adapt the world to himself. Therefore, all progress depends on the unreasonable man."

GEORGE BERNARD SHAW, IRISH DRAMATIST

Traditionally, leaders are paid to be right. In turn, they have a vested interest in making sure their opinions prevail. Most often these traditional leaders do not take pleasure in being contradicted. In our experience we have found that leaders (especially traditional ones) are annoyed by disagreements or resistance. Unfortunately this restrained approach is exactly the opposite mindset than that needed for a leader to achieve in today's business environment. Leaders can no longer just tolerate diverse thinking; they must actively seek it and think as a resilient Agile Business Leader. They must be able to lead through the constant seismic shifts of the organization.

Resilience is defined as a staunch acceptance of reality. Resilient people typically have strongly held values and an uncanny ability to improvise and adapt to significant change. Resilient leaders are relatively good at developing an accurate assessment of a situation and being able to move forward with getting bogged down. Nonresilient people are prone to blame others or themselves for their failures.

The concept of resilience has to do with the ability to bend, stretch, compress, and return back to your original shape or position. For example, after being stretched, a rubber band returns to its original shape when the tension on it is released. Being resilient as a leader means being able to bend, stretch, and absorb change gracefully while retaining core values and functions. One leader we spoke with told us, "I have to mediate my emotions, I know that. So after my tantrum, I become an adult again." The qualities of agility and flexibility enable leaders to be resilient and recover quickly and reliably when they are stressed or thrown off balance by change or adversity.

Resilient leaders draw on their ability to be optimistic, which allows them to function well in difficult situations. They have an abundant reserve of centeredness, innovation, and stamina.

Being centered refers to being emotionally stable and secure. This centeredness enables leaders to keep balance when turbulent times knock them around. When ABL leaders are centered, they are poised and levelheaded, especially under stress. They feel calm, composed, and completely present.

Being innovative refers to the ability and power to create solutions of value. When leaders are innovative they express themselves with imagination and originality. They envision new possibilities and respond to novel situations with flexibility and improvisation.

Having stamina refers to the physical and moral strength required to sustain prolonged stressful efforts or activities along with the ability to withstand hardship or adversity, disease, and unexpected change. When you have an abundance of stamina, you feel invigorated and confident in your ability to endure.

Resilient leaders who are centered will be innovative, and their stamina increases their capacity to thrive regardless of the situation swirling around them. Champions are able to recover quickly from illness, change, or misfortune. The ability to perform and thrive under conditions of ambiguity and uncertainty is essential for resilient Agile Business Leaders.

From a biological perspective, humans are quite resilient. When we get frightened, our body gives us a shot of performance-enhancing hormones and pumps blood to our limbs to help us out-run whatever enemy we face. It has been found that people who respond well to trauma and are resilient to the adversities of disasters tend to have three underlying advantages:

1. A belief that they can influence events.

2. An ability to find meaningful purpose in life's turmoil.

3. A conviction that they can learn from positive and negative experiences.

Champions recognize their natural ability to be resilient and can adapt in the face of adversity, significantly influencing the situation and alleviating the sources of stress. They are able to bounce back from workplace and personal stressors.

AGILE ANALOGY

Eileen remembers the story of one of the most frightening experiences of her life and how she quickly learned to be resilient during and after experiencing danger.

My most frightening experience was when I was a cashier at a department store and a man came in, held a sawed-off shotgun up to my face, and demanded money from the cash register. I was nineteen years old at the time and working during the Christmas holidays at a large retail store. The area of the store where I worked was packed with people, and the man with the gun began yelling at me to put the money in the bag. Clearly, I did not want this man to harm anyone. He was agitated and nervous, and I knew terrible consequences were possible. As I began to open the cash register, he screamed louder, shaking the shotgun in my face and demanding that I hurry up. I began to talk to the man smoothly and calmly (I have no idea how I did that), saying that I would do as he asked and he would get what he wanted. I removed the money from the drawer and filled his bag. The people in the store looked with horror as the event unfolded. The man took the bag, turned around, and with the gun pointing in the air, demanded that no one should move.

Immediately after the man left, I called the police and then checked with the customers to make sure everyone was all right. After the police came, we reviewed mug shots, and they commented on my calmness and ability to capture some of the details of the robber. I was on a mission to catch this person and knew providing every bit of possible information to the police would be helpful in apprehending him.

After the robbery and review of all the mug shots, I went home. It wasn't until I was sitting on my couch in my home that I began to shake when the internal realization of what had happened hit me. Somehow, during the events of the robbery, I was able to communicate effectively, keep people calm, perform under stress, and manage strong feelings and the impulse to scream and pass out. The next day I was back at work, wiser and more alert to my surroundings. We also put new procedures in place to help manage how much money was kept in the cash register at any one time.

Resilience is about the ability to bounce back quickly. How much resilience a person has at any given moment can make the difference between a leader experiencing a particular situation as painfully challenging or as an open-ended opportunity for personal growth—or even an adventure. In dealing with and managing turmoil, a leader must act quickly. Resilience under the threat of turmoil or chaos is a function of speed, decision-making, action, reaction, collaboration, and swiftly applied common sense. Timidity and hesitation are not options. Truly resilient leaders do not just recover and return back to exactly what they were before the chaos occurred. Instead, they add to their knowledge reservoir and increase their resilience capability.

RECOVERY, LEARNING   RESILIENCE

The key to staying successful as a leader, despite the challenges and chaos in business, is finding ways to bounce back. Resilient leaders are able to solve problems with a calm, confident sense of being able to overcome adversity. They approach challenges with agility and learn from each experience (both positively and negatively).

We recommend the following approaches for developing resilience:

Focus on Succeeding

- Focus on opportunities, not obstacles.
- Expect that good things can happen despite adversity.
- Exert positive influence to create positive outcomes.
- Be clear about what matters most.
- Stay focused: value-driven, not event-driven.
- Solicit feedback to understand reality from multiple perspectives.

Strengthen Mental Abilities

- Renew physical energy through periodic recovery time.

- Develop emotional empathy and self-awareness.

- Learn greater self-control to manage strong feelings and impulses.

- Expect the world to be disruption-filled.

- Learn to steady concentration to manage adversity.

Expand Thinking

- Build and maintain supportive and positive relationships.

- Develop the capacity to make and implement realistic plans.

- Evaluate and affirm strengths and abilities.

- Enrich skills in communication and problem solving.

- Increase the ability to respond in a positive and decisive manner.

- Develop a high tolerance for ambiguity, paradox, and complexity.

- Celebrate small wins.

The Resilient Question

The list above supports the competencies of the ABL Champion and our thinking about being resilient. In the role of Champion, leaders who have this competency do not use it to get bogged down and chained up by restrictions; instead they become more resilient and able to quickly bounce back from any disruptions that might occur. They have the ability to be flexible, step back to gain perspective, be more adaptable, and rebound well from diversities.

Building the habit of resilience helps a Champion to elegantly weather the unavoidable ups and downs of the business environment. The Champion is resilient and seeks out new opportunities even in times of crisis, easily answering the question, "How can I bounce back from periods of stress and times of chaos?"

THEORY IN PRACTICE ACTIVITY 3.7

GOOD POINT!

Objective of this exercise: To create the ability to thrive no matter what life puts in your path. Through the use of quotes, this exercise has you self-reflect and adjust your thinking on current situations. It helps you move toward being more resilient by deciding how to bounce back from setbacks and become motivated to overcome challenges.

Instructions: Read each of the quotes below and state how that specific quote offers important learning for your role as a leader. What has this quote reminded you to keep doing? After reading this quote, what action are you inspired to do moving forward?

1. *"We often refuse to accept an idea merely because the tone of voice in which it has been expressed is unsympathetic to us."* (Friedrich Nietzsche).

How is this quote an important lesson for my role as a leader?

Remember to: _____

From now on I will: _____

2. *"No matter how cynical I get, I just can't keep up."* (Nora Ephron).

How is this quote an important lesson for my role as a leader?

Remember to: _____

From now on I will: _____

3. *"The man who fights too long against dragons becomes a dragon himself."* (Friedrich Nietzsche).

How is this quote an important lesson for my role as a leader?

Remember to: _____

From now on I will: _____

4. *"I am learning all the time. The tombstone will be my diploma."* (Eartha Kitt).

How is this quote an important lesson for my role as a leader?

Remember to: _____

From now on I will: _____

5. *"We adore chaos because we love to produce order."*

(M. C. Escher).

How is this quote an important lesson for my role as a leader?

Remember to: _____

From now on I will: _____

6. *"What matters now isn't individual empowerment. It's collaborative advantage"* (Warren Bennis).

How is this quote an important lesson for my role as a leader?

Remember to: _____

From now on I will: _____

7. *"Be joyful though you have considered all the facts."* (Wendell Berry).

How is this quote an important lesson for my role as a leader?

Remember to: _____

From now on I will: _____

8. *"Brooks' Law says there is an incremental person who, when added to a project, makes it take more, not less time. Remember, nine women can't make a baby in one month."* (Fred Brooks).

How is this quote an important lesson for my role as a leader?

Remember to: _____

From now on I will: _____

9. *"No man ever steps into the same river twice, for it's not the same river and he's not the same man."* (Heraclitus).

How is this quote an important lesson for my role as a leader?

Remember to: _____

From now on I will: _____

10. *"Those who cannot remember the past are condemned to repeat it."* (George Santayana).

How is this quote an important lesson for my role as a leader?

Remember to: _____

From now on I will: _____

11. *"Age is a case of mind over matter. If you don't mind, it don't matter."* (Satchel Paige).

How is this quote an important lesson for my role as a leader?

Remember to: _____

From now on I will: _____

12. *"An ant may well destroy a whole dam."* (Chinese proverb).

How is this quote an important lesson for my role as a leader?

Remember to: _____

From now on I will: _____

13. *"The greatest problem with communication is the illusion that it has been accomplished."* (George Bernard Shaw).

How is this quote an important lesson for my role as a leader?

Remember to: _____

From now on I will: _____

14. *"We evoke a potential that is already present."* (Margaret Wheatly).

How is this quote an important lesson for my role as a leader?

Remember to: _____

From now on I will: _____

10

CHAMPION COMPETENCY #5

▲ Practice Work/Life Balance ▼

Champions are true to personal values and are not driven solely by financial gain, recognition, or even power. They are ruthless at prioritizing and recognizing what is important and what can wait. They know when to stop, when to say no, and when mental health and physical health need to be restored.

The concept of work/life balance has made time a valuable and limited resource to be shared between the organization and the people. Businesses are generally organized to achieve business goals in the most time-efficient manner possible. Performance is judged by results, not by availability of staff, the number of hours worked, or physical presence at work. Both the length of the work-day and the workweek are at issue. The Champion must work with the reality that globalization has changed work schedules, making it possible for him to work twenty-four hours a day, seven days a week. The result of the work/life cocktail is a workaholic culture in which work/life balance and personal health have been significantly impacted.

Our thoughts about work, leisure, health, and balancing it all have taken on new forms and rules. Physical location of the employee has largely become irrelevant when it comes to work these days. iPads, BlackBerry's, globalization, rising energy concerns, and economic pressures have shifted telecommuting into a more common way for people to work.

In the 1960s and 1970s in North America, employers considered work/life balance mainly an issue for working mothers who struggled with work demands, raising children, and managing a household. In the 1980s, the concept of work/life balance became an issue for both men and women, precipitated by the development of corporate policies and governmental laws regarding maternity leave, parental leave, employee assistance programs, flextime, adoption assistance, child and elder care assistance, and work-at-home options. In the 1990s, people began making job choices based on the "work/life balance culture" of the organization. Employees chose the company that best suited how they wanted to live and work. Now in the twenty-first century, leaders face issues of personal stress, more limited resources, health-care costs, differences in generational work ethic, globalization, 24/7 accessible information, outsourcing, and investor expectations as impacting the management of work/life balance. Work and personal life have become increasingly interconnected and integrated as technology enables people to work anywhere at any time. Work comes home (emails at night), and personal lives come to work (personal responsibilities, appointments, phone calls).

A study at the University of Oregon found, "Telecommuting is a growing trend in the information age. Much has been published touting the benefits of the "'virtual office.'" About 6 percent of the American workforce (over 8 million American workers) telecommute to company jobs from their homes on either a part-time or full-time basis, and the number is increasing. By some estimates, a full 30 percent of the workforce will be telecommuting by the year 2020." Even the U.S. Congress has recognized the shift and created the Telework Enhancement Act of 2010:

(Retrieved September 24, 2011 from http://hr.uoregon.edu/policy/telecommuting.html)

President Obama signed the Telework Enhancement Act of 2010, providing agencies greater flexibility in managing our workforce. The Act provides a framework for agencies to better leverage technology and to maximize the use of flexible work arrangements, which will aid in recruiting new Federal workers, retain valuable talent and allow the Federal government to maintain productivity in various situations—including those involving national security and other emergency situations.

To maximize the impact of this new law, OPM will be coordinating agency efforts to build effective telework programs with three key objectives in mind:

1. **Improve Continuity of Operations (COOP)**—using telework as a strategy to keep government operational during inclement weather or other emergencies.

2. **Promote Management Effectiveness**—using telework to target reductions in management costs related to employee turnover and absenteeism, and to reduce real estate costs and environmental impact and transit costs.

3. **Enhance Work-Life Balance**—using telework to allow employees to better manage their work and family obligations, retaining a more resilient Federal workforce able to better meet agency goals.

(Source: U.S. Office of Personnel Management and the Chief Human Capital Officers [CHCO] Council Retrieved September 23, 2011 from http://www.chcoc.gov/transmittals/TransmittalDetails.aspx?Trans mittalID=3246)

Practicing work/life balance is an important competency for leaders. It is linked to successful leaders and how they value the work and the quality of their work, along with how they value the time and the quality of their personal life. In short, there's no dollar sign on piece of mind!

Author Tom Peters while speaking at the Executive Forum and told staffing executives that it was stupid to have their white-collar managers watching the behavior and managing their employees—he suggested that microprocessors should be doing that. The reality is that in many companies business rules are embedded in software systems that monitor key business drivers and conditions and proactively guide and direct the employees to successful behaviors. We have seen a number of our clients in the staffing industry successfully apply this technology and believe that in the next 10 years it will become a much more popular way to optimize the performance of a staffing business. Two major advantages of leveraging intelligent systems: (1) Intelligent systems have the ability to watch, correct and prompt best practices in real time vs. a human manager who cannot be seeing everything that is going on at the same time. … [And (2)], it frees managers to be concentrating their energies on higher, hopefully more revenue-generating, activities.

(Source: Staffingindustry.com)

(Retrieved September 24, 2011 from
http://www.staffingindustry.com/Research-
Publications/Publications/SI-Review/January-2011/2020-
Customers-Technology-Forecast)

Socrates said, "Beware the barrenness of a busy life." We suggest
that this shift in where a person works also comes with a need for
discipline and separating time (mentally and physically) spent
working and relaxing for the goal of achieving work/life balance.

Tom Kosnik, a consulting professor who teaches global entrepreneurial marketing and the Entrepreneurial Thought Leaders Semi-
nar in the Stanford Technology Ventures Program at the Stanford
University School of Engineering, listed the top ten trends for 2020
that clearly will have an impact on work/life balance.

1. Work tasks will continue to be dissected and redesigned.

2. Technology and the Internet will support telecommuting,
    outsourcing, work from home, work from another country,
    a dispersed workforce.

3. The values of people entering the workforce in the United
    States will continue to shift and become less "work" orien-
    tated and more "quality" orientated.

4. Outsourcing and off-shoring will continue; multinationals
    will have to import and train human capital or set up shop
    in developing nations.

5. Population and ethnic group growth rates will change the
    makeup of the workforce, and the staffing industry will
    have to respond fittingly.

6. More companies, small and larger, will employ the aging population and will alter the workplace to do so.

7. The staffing industry will continue to grow.

8. New low-cost staffing business models will continue to emerge.

9. National staffing firms will take more of the staffing revenue pie.

10. Independents will find it more and more difficult to make money in their business. (Source: Staffingindustry.com)

This new reality of how individuals work and balance the mix between work and personal life makes the challenges of work/life balance an issue that leaders must work with and resolve.

AGILE ILLUSTRATION

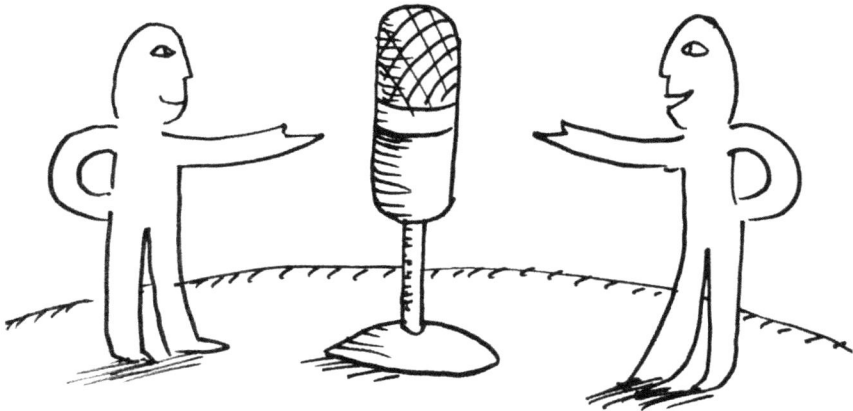

One executive Eileen coached at Vonage (a provider of broadband telephone services) came to realize that he had an issue with work/life balance during one of their coaching sessions. Vonage was in its early stages of growing. As with many startups, everyone worked long hours to get everything done. Commitment to achieve the impossible was the driving force for everyone working there. As the company grew, employees and leaders continued to be charged by the adrenaline rush they received from solving problems and innovating new features to their product. After three years, these intense work/life habits and the thrill of the rush became the norm. Eileen's coaching client began to realize that this work habit was having negative impact on his marriage and on his family life.

During dinner with my daughter and wife, my BlackBerry kept ringing, and I know I need to respond to it, so I do. My wife isn't happy. At 3 a.m. I'm lying in bed responding to emails on my "crackberry" while my wife is sleeping beside me. Every minute of my day is work focused. We want to have another child, but my wife is concerned about that. She has given me an ultimatum: balance my life or go live at the company. I am choosing to balance my life.

Eileen and he talked about some of the issues driving him to work as he did and how his constant focus on work was impacting his health, marriage, family life, and work performance. They came up with a plan. Part of the plan involved him putting his BlackBerry into a drawer every night at 9 p.m. He committed to not looking at his BlackBerry from 9 p.m. to 6:30 a.m. He knew even this small start was needed to begin to change his behavior and his focus. He also wanted to do something that could be achieved easily. How hard could this be?

On the first night of his mini–work/life balance mission, Eileen (a committed coach) called his BlackBerry at 9:30 p.m., and he answered it! She "urged" him to put the BlackBerry in the drawer and enjoy the rest of his evening. On the second night, she called his BlackBerry at 10:00 p.m., and there was no answer. The next day he emailed her saying that he just went to check who was calling him and smiled when he saw her name come up on caller ID. He chose not to answer it. He was getting the message and changing his habits. From that point on, the BlackBerry stayed in the drawer at night. Anyone who really needed to reach him knew his personal cell phone and home numbers and could call if it was really necessary and an immediate response was needed. Coworkers and staff were aware of his work/life balance goal and not only respected his thinking, but they also recognized that the behavior he was modeling was to help them with their own work/life balance as well. Eileen's client found that he now works better and is happier because of the balanced approach. (As a side note, the next year, he and his wife had their second child. Congratulations!)

If someone invests every bit of time and energy into a job, it may have the unintended consequence of making that person dependent on the job for everything, including a sense of personal worth. The Champion is aware that the pace, predictability, and complexity that a job carries with it offer the potential for burnout. A Champion recognizes that organizational objectives and individual work/life objectives are not an either/or choice. When organizations and leaders focus on the employees' well-being and stress reduction, they are not only helping each person, they are also making a strategic organizational decision to improve performance. Stress impairs the immune system and the memory, and it also inhibits learning because it encourages routine rather than creative responses.

AGILE ILLUSTRATION

In 1979 Eileen worked at Norwall, a leading Canadian manufacturer of wallpaper. The CEO at the time was Derek Ashton. Derek had an uncommon idea for designing his company. He viewed health and recreation as the keys to an employee's well-being and performance on the assembly lines. He hired Eileen as a full-time industrial "recreologist" to work with employees and "assist them in developing meaningful leisure pursuits." She ran recreational activities in the company's personalized recreation center in order to promote healthy lifestyles for team building, fun, and mental well-being. Eileen remembers . . .

> Back in 1979 this was an unusual concept for an organization. Most firms focused on work only. We made sure our employees had fun, too. One day I remember Derek coming back from a business trip to Australia and telling us this wild story. He said if we thought having a fitness center in our company was different, then what did we think about Australian hotels having fitness rooms as part of the facility where guests could work out on treadmills, exercise bikes,

and weight machines. We couldn't believe our ears at this strange tale Derek told us about life in another part of the world. Little did we know how much of an expected norm this concept would become in the future and how important this service would become for personal health.

The length of both the workday and the workweek, and workload are all at issue in the pursuit of reaching balance. Champions bring heart, mind, and hands to work and effectively navigate work and personal life simultaneously, deliver results collaboratively, create new knowledge, challenge existing ways of doing things, and work well under diverse arrangements. They are efficient with how they expend their energy and attention, and they know when enough is enough. Champions can say no when they have to. They can integrate the various aspects of their lives and bring all of who they are to achieve the organization's goals without compromising personal needs. The Champion can establish boundaries and distinguish between work and private life.

AGILE ANALOGY

Work/life balance is not only a physical and daily calendar issue; it is also a concept that involves mental attitude and biology. Below are two analogies on the biological and attitudinal impacts of work-life balance.

Biological Impact

Douglas Madsen found in his research a substantial correlation between blood serotonin levels and certain personality characteristics. Serotonin, a neurotransmitter in the body, contributes to feelings of well-being and happiness.

He assessed a group to determine if they had a Type A behavior pattern and asked those in the study to rate the following comments.

Type A Behavior Pattern

Aggressiveness

I lose patience with speakers who don't get to the point.

I get a bit angry with people who can't understand simple ideas.

It makes me angry when people are late for appointments.

Drive

I probably eat faster than I should.

After eating, I want to get busy instead of sitting around.

Competitiveness

I am more responsible than most college students.

I often set deadlines for myself.

I need to slow down, to be less active.

I plan to find a career that is difficult and challenging.

I am more precise than most people.

I find competition stimulating.

Other

Everyday life is filled with challenges to be met.

I stay up late at night to relax and unwind.

I am relaxed and easygoing.

When I do a job, I do it well.

My friends see me as competitive and hard driving.

Frequently I think of other things when someone is talking to me.

I like to get up and get going in the morning.

I give more effort to my work than do most.

I am more serious than most people.

Internal-External Control

I do not believe that luck plays an important part in my life.

When I make plans, I am almost certain I can make them work.

Most people's lives are controlled by chance circumstances.

I have more willpower than most people seem to have.

Anxiety

Normally I feel secure.

Sometimes I feel useless.

Much of the time, I feel under stress.

Normally I feel calm.

Normally I feel a little bit anxious.

Normally I feel self-confident.

Often I feel worried.

General

I would dislike being a member of a leaderless group.

Strong leaders are what made this country great.

People can be trusted.

Once I make up my mind I seldom change it.

I have less energy than most people my age.

In the end, Madsen found that individuals who were highly driven and who had aggressive, competitive, and hard-charging personalities had substantially higher serotonin levels in their blood than individuals who scored low on these personality characteristics.

The study investigated changes in serotonin levels when a person had a change in status: dominant individuals who become nondominant exhibit a decline in serotonin, and nondominant individuals who become dominant show the reverse. In other words, if a dominant person loses power or status, a sense of well-being is also lost. And if a nondominant person gains status, a sense of well-being is also lost.

(Retrieved September 16, 2001 from http://ir.uiowa.edu/cgi/viewcontent.cgi?article=1041&context=poli sci_pubs&sei-redir=1#search=%22Douglas%20Madsen%20 Whole%20Blood%20Serotonin%20Leadership%22)

What does this mean for work-life balance and the Agile Business Leader? It turns out that competitiveness, drive, and self-confidence as part of your personality determine how you manage your work-life balance.

AGILE ANALOGY

Attitudinal Impact

Work/life balance is also about being present and conscious, and knowing how to achieve happiness. Stable, happy employees lead to stable, happy customers. At this point we are not suggesting that the Champion is a Pollyanna with uncontained optimism and a tendency to find good in everything and be happy, happy all the time. At the same time, we are suggesting that some lessons can be learned from Eleanor Porter and her character Pollyanna.

In Porter's story, Pollyanna Whittier is an orphan who goes to live with her strict Aunt Polly. Aunt Polly is not prepared for a child with infectious energy and determination who sees the best in every situation. Pollyanna makes everyone she encounters happier as a result of their meeting. When Pollyanna meets a problem, she plays the "glad game":

"'Oh, yes, in the glad game you just find something about everything to be glad about—no matter what 'twas,' rejoined Pollyanna, earnestly."

(Retrieved February 19, 2010 from
http://www.classicreader.com/book/1368/5/)

Pollyanna's approach to life led to the development of the Pollyanna Principle, or Pollyannaism, which describes a tendency for people to hear only the positive statements. It is synonymous with people wanting to "hear no evil, see no evil, speak no evil, and believe no evil."

So what does this attitudinal impact mean for work-life balance and the Agile Business Leader? It means balance is achieved through accepting and dealing with the reality of the situation and awareness of what impact that situation has on your health and your time.

Champions must respect how imperative it is to provide people, including themselves, with the means to attain a healthy work/life balance in the complex life of juggling work, family, friendships, interests, and obligations from a very real perspective.

One of our clients, Novozymes North America, has been recognized by the North Carolina Psychological Association as a psychologically healthy workplace. The criteria for this award include work environment, culture, initiative, flextime, and work/life balance. Novozyme intentionally aligned its corporate values with a work/life balance. The entire culture has embraced this conviction, and everyone is considered part of the solution.

Champions do not fall victim to Pollyannaism. Instead they recognize that everyone in the organization is responsible for finding a solution to the issue of work/life balance, and everyone's situation is to be respected.

The personal consequences of work/life imbalance are well docu-mented, including:

- Increased levels of stress and stress-related illnesses.

- Lower life satisfaction.

- Higher rates of family strife, violence, and divorce.

- Rising incidence of substance abuse.

- Growing problems with parenting and supervision of chil-dren and adolescents.

- Escalating rates of juvenile delinquency and violence.

The negative consequences for work/life imbalance on the organization are also substantial. They can lead to:

- Higher rates of absenteeism and turnover.

- Reduced productivity.

- Decreased job satisfaction.

- Lower levels of organizational commitment and loyalty.

- Rising health-care costs.

(Retrieved September 16, 2011 from
http://www.allbusiness.com/specialty-businesses/home-based-businesses-work/752639-1.html).

Consistent with the findings from the good Samaritan research, Levine found that, in general, the cities with the fastest pace of life were the least helpful. Rochester, New York, which had a relatively slow pace of life for a northeastern city, was rated the most helpful city in America. New York City, ranked third in terms of pace of life, was rated the least helpful city in America. There were notable exceptions, however. California cities typically had slow paces of life but were consistently rated as less helpful than faster cities. Thus, a slower pace of life may be a necessary but insufficient condition for altruism. Californians may have the time to help others but may be more interested in helping themselves to the good life.

Levine's research teams visit cities and measure walking speeds, clock accuracy, and the tempo of basic business transactions such as buying stamps at the post office. From these metrics, Levine has calculated the pace of life in dozens of cities around the world. Western European countries lead the world in rapid pace of life, with Switzerland at the top of the list. Japan is also high on the index. Second-world countries are found predominantly at the bottom of the list. Of thirty-one countries measured, Mexico has the slowest pace of life. In the United States, Boston, New York, and other northeastern cities lead the list as the fastest cities in America, while southern and western cities are the slowest. Los Angeles is the slowest of all.

AGILE ILLUSTRATION

To expand on the topic of work/life balance, we spoke with our client Jeremy Gwee. Jeremy has an extensive career in the financial industry, spanning thirty years. He is currently working with HSBC, one of the largest banking and financial services organizations in the world. We asked Jeremy for his perspective as his department had high engagement scores for work/life balance in a recent survey.

I became more aware of the importance of work/life balance after the bank's first Global People Survey in 2007. I must admit that, before that, I took work/life balance for granted because in all the previous organizations I worked for, there was no formal feedback of this kind. The survey caused me to reexamine my approach to work/life balance because not only was it management's concern, but the staff also responded seriously.

We cannot dispute the fact that not all of us work because we like to work. For many of us, working for a living is perhaps the main reason that we work. If there is a choice not to work, I believe many would opt for that choice. But life is what it is. Most of us are brought up not to value work, but rather to work because there is no other means to survive. In each one of us, we recognize that there are competing desires in our lives. There are other things that we prefer to do. We cannot help but feel lost and anxious about what tomorrow may bring. Each day when we appear at work, we bring along our anxieties, our personal circumstances, and our personal obligations. Each day we have to strike a balance between this mental state and the work that lies before us. How can we be productive and earn our keep honestly?

As a leader I may not be in a position to help every employee manage his or her anxieties, personal circumstances, and obligations. But I believe that I can improve their work/life balance if I can create a work environment that empathizes with their challenges. There is a certain quote I read from Confucius that I believe has convinced me of this: "A man of humanity is one who, in seeking to establish himself, finds a foothold for others and who, desiring attainment for himself, helps others to attain." Management has expectations of us as leaders, but that should not always translate into cracking of the whip. For example, introducing flexible work hours can create some space for employees to meet their personal obligations. Making it comfortable for employees to leave early without feeling guilty, as long as the work is done, allows employees to be able to make use of what is left of the day. Our employees are highly educated, and they have aspirations; let us respect that and do what we can to promote their aspirations.

As leaders we will be exhausted if we are expected to always make our employees happy. But organizations should consider equipping employees, as part of their development program, with work/life management skills to help them navigate through life. Without employees having such skills, how can we expect them to come to work and be ready to be part of a team? While not wanting to be accused of advocating that employers play the role of nanny, it is nevertheless unavoidable because people cannot leave their private lives at the workplace door from nine to five. Work/life balance skills are unfortunately not taught in schools. Employees, as an organization's human capital, are important to corporate success. Leaders must enable people to move from dependent and independent employee relationships to more interdependent and teamwork relationships.

I think work/life balance begins with a person's own life. I'm reminded by the quote from Czechoslovakian playwright-politician Václav Havel, who said, "Whether all is really lost or not depends entirely on whether I am lost." If our employees feel lost, how can they be expected to be proactive as described in Stephen Covey's *Seven Habits for Highly Effective People*? If they feel lost, then how are they going to be responsible for their attitudes and actions? How are they going to be able to respond and be responsible for their action? Perhaps work/life balance begins with us helping our employees to find themselves, prioritize their life goals, and take responsibility.

What industry you work in, what organization you work for, and what colleagues you work with all have an impact on your work/life balance. As it turns out, what city you live in also impacts how fast you walk and get things done. Jason Collins [writes in his blog that there is a strong relationship between the size of cities and the residents' speed of walking. The larger the city, the quicker its residents scamper from A to B. A number of studies have confirmed this relationship and have broadened the relationship to the speed of other activities (such as betel nuts changing hands quicker in Port Moresby than in rural centers in Papua New Guinea).

To manage work/life balance, some offices provide flextime, a benefit that reduces the rigidity of set office hours and enables staff to adjust their working day. Flextime works within certain limits, according to personal choice and convenience, and at the same time improves service to customers. Other companies offer virtual offices as a way of maintaining work/life balance. All these options are great, except that the clock still ticks when you are not there, and your actions as an employee still affect your coworkers. We are all part of a greater whole. When it comes to work/life balance, in the words of philosopher Eric Hoffer, "In this time of dramatic change, it's the learners who will inherit the future. The learned will find themselves equipped to live in a world that no longer exists." The leaders who help people "think to think" and consider different angles with no perfect point for an answer: these are the ones who will achieve work/life balance.

THEORY IN PRACTICE ACTIVITY 3.8

INCREASE YOUR PERSONAL WATTAGE

Objective of this exercise: To quickly and graphically identify the areas in your life to which you want to devote more energy, and to help you understand where you might want to cut back.

Instructions:

Step 1: Brainstorm the number of roles you perform in your life: For example; husband/wife, father/mother, sister/brother, leader, manager, colleague, team member, community leader, caregiver, artist, student, friend, and so on.

_____   _____   _____

_____   _____   _____

_____   _____   _____

_____   _____   _____

_____   _____   _____

_____   _____   _____

Step 2: From the list created in Step 1, choose the top six roles that consume most of your energy—not *time*, but *energy*. These are roles that you think most often about because you know you must perform them well, or the roles you put the most amount of effort toward, or the roles that consume your thoughts regularly. If you would like to choose more than six, that is OK. We suggest you do not choose more than eight top roles for this Theory in Practice Activity.

Top Six Roles
1.
2.
3.
4.
5.
6.
7. (optional)
8. (optional)

Step 3: On a scale of 0 (low) to 5 (high), write down the amount of energy you are exerting in that area of your life.

Top Six Roles	*Amount of Energy Exerted* *0 (low) to 5 (high)*
1.	
2.	
3.	
4.	
5.	
6.	
7. (optional)	
8. (optional)	

Step 4: Assign a percentage amount to each of the roles so that all six (or seven or eight) roles total 100 percent.

Top Six Roles	Amount of Energy exerted 0 (low) to 5 (high)	Percentage of Energy Exerted
1.		
2.		
3.		
4.		
5.		
6.		
7. (optional)		
8. (optional)		
TOTAL:		**100%**

Step 5: Using the Current Energy Wheel following, divide the wheel into sections to represent the percentages you have assigned each of your six (or more) roles. For example, if your roles are Driver to Kids' Events 20%, Parent 15%, Volunteer 15%, Leader 40%, Friend 5%, and Spouse 5%, your wheel might look like the example given.

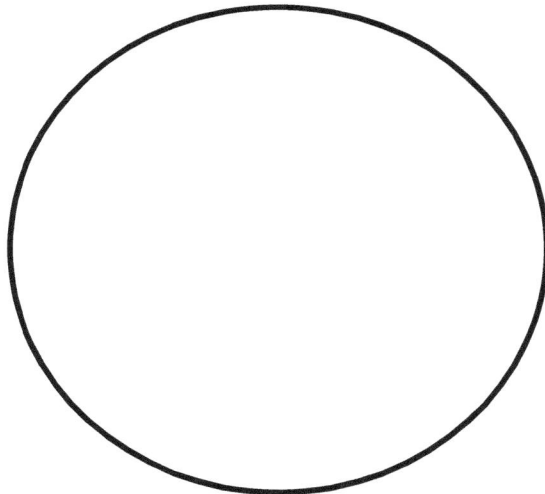

Current Energy Wheel

Step 6: Review and assess your Current Energy Wheel. Are these the percentages you want to place on each of these roles? Are these the top roles on which you would like to be expending the most amount of your energy?

Step 7: Adjust your list of roles to represent how you want to be expending your energy and efforts. If you have good work/life balance, your top roles and how much energy would you be exerting toward each role?

Desired Top Six Roles	Amount of Energy Exerted 0 (low) to 5 (high)
1.	
2.	
3.	
4.	
5.	
6.	
7. (optional)	
8. (optional)	

Step 8: As you did in Step 4, assign a percentage amount to each of the roles so that all six (or seven or eight) roles total 100 percent.

Desired Top Six Roles	Amount of Energy exerted 0 (low) to 5 (high)	Percentage of Energy Exerted
1.		
2.		
3.		
4.		
5.		
6.		
7. (optional)		
8. (optional)		
TOTAL:		**100%**

Step 9: Using the Desired Energy Wheel following, divide the wheel into sections to represent the percentages you have assigned each of your new desired six (or more) roles.

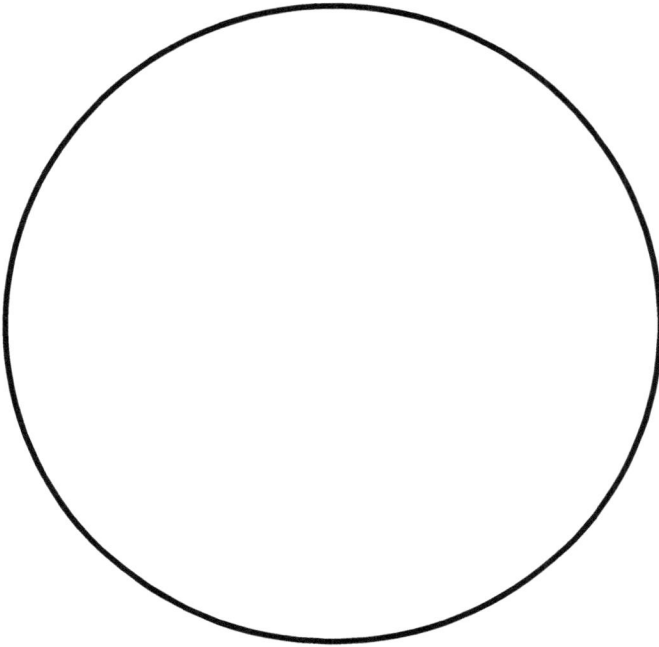

Desired Energy Wheel

Step 10: Once you have created your new Energy Wheel, plan the actions needed to work on regaining balance.

1. What action or activities do you need to start doing to regain balance?

_____

2. How can you redirect your current energy to reach the percentages of your Desired Energy Wheel?

_____

3. What activities or roles can you eliminate, reprioritize, or delegate to someone else to help achieve your Desired Energy Wheel?

_____

4. How can you transform the knowledge you have gained from this Theory in Practice Activity to turn your work/life balance into a habit?

_____

5. What commitments are you willing to make to ensure that you achieve your Desired Energy Wheel?

_____

Champions use all of their talents and wisdom to reach a personal Mount Everest. They know that having the ability to clarify and establish what is most important in life will allow for the allocation of the appropriate amount of energy to each situation. Champions are not scattered in every direction and lost among multiple needs, desires, and interests. They have learned how to differentiate likes from needs.

11

CHAMPION TRAIT #4

▲ Committed ▼

"There is no action without desire,
for it is desire that causes us to act."

ARISTOTLE

Organizational commitment and optimism are fundamental to Agile Business Leaders. In our experience, we find that commitment to the organization has a great consequence for business and, more importantly, can be strongly impacted by the way leaders work with employees. The old psychological contract between an organization and employees—the one where employers provide job security and predictable advancement to employees in exchange for their loyalty and performance—has been damaged beyond repair. Organizational commitment is being challenged by employees who are more attached to their profession than to their organization and apply greater discretionary effort on to what and to whom they will be committed.

This ABL trait of commitment is about attachment to a cause, including its goals, values, and purpose. We believe commitment affects a leader's performance on the job, her intent to leave or stay on task, and the amount of effort she is willing to put toward an outcome.

SERVICE & COMMITMENT to others is the RENT we Pay FOR LIVING ON This Earth...

Some people that believe service and commitment to others are the rent we pay for living on this Earth. We believe that these leaders are the ones who are positioning themselves as strategic, highly impactful business partners.

AGILE ILLUSTRATION

An impressive example of how commitment can strengthen an outcome comes from the story of W. N. Murray. Murray was an avid Scottish mountain-climbing enthusiast who joined the Scottish Division of the British Army during World War II. While in the war, he spent three years in prisoner-of-war camps in Italy, Germany, and Czechoslovakia. With his commitment to and passion for mountain climbing, Murray wrote a book about it while in the terrible conditions of the war camps. He wrote his book, *Mountaineering In Scotland*, on rough toilet paper, the only paper he had available. His manuscript was found by the Gestapo and destroyed. Murray did not give up hope. He was committed to his cause, and to the surprise of his fellow prisoners, he started to write the book again.

After the end of the war, Murray's commitment not only helped him publish his first book but several others as well. He is known in history as the person who rejuvenated the postwar interest in mountain climbing. Not only did Murray write his book but he was also a deputy leader to the climbers on a Mount Everest expedition. Unfortunately, Murray failed to acclimatize to the altitude and was no longer included on the successive teams. Being unable to achieve a dream did not stop Murray from sharing it with others through his writing.

WHATEVER YOU CAN DO, OR DREAM YOU CAN DO... BEGIN IT...

In one of his books, Murray writes about commitment and the courage to continue with the cause even when things seem lost. His lessons are very relevant to the Champion:

> But when I said that nothing had been done I erred in one important matter. We had definitely committed ourselves and were halfway out of our ruts. We had put down our passage money—booked a sailing to Bombay. This may sound too simple, but is great in consequence. Until one is committed, there is hesitancy, the chance to draw back, always ineffectiveness. Concerning all acts of initiative (and creation), there is one elementary truth, the ignorance of which kills countless ideas and splendid plans: that the moment one definitely commits oneself, then providence moves too. A whole stream of events issues from the decision, raising in one's favor all manner of unforeseen incidents, meetings and material assistance, which no man could have dreamt would have come his way. I learned a deep respect for one of Goethe's couplets:
>
> Whatever you can do or dream you can, begin it.
> Boldness has genius, power and magic in it!

(W.N. Murray, The Scottish Himalayan Expedition, 1951)

(Retrieved February 19, 2010 from
http://www.goethesociety.org/pages/quotescom.html)

When commitment exists and a leader believes and accepts the goals and values of the purpose, then that leader is willing to exert considerable effort on behalf of the cause and the organization. But where does commitment come from, and how can you achieve it?

AGILE ANALOGY

There is a theory that one's commitment level is based on biology. Psychologist Peter Hall of Waterloo University in Ontario, Canada, found a connection between commitment and behavior that lies in the neurons of the brain (more specifically the prefrontal cortex, which is the front of the brain, located right beneath the forehead). The cortex is responsible for mediating conflicting thoughts, making choices between right and wrong, helping you decide on a defined goal, and having social control to manage outcomes. During his research, Hall gave participants the Stroop test, an electronic test in which names of colors flash on the screen for an instant, but are aligned with the "wrong" colors. For example, the word "red" would be written in green letters and the world "blue" would be written in yellow letters. The purpose of the test is for the person to quickly identify the color of the letters. The test is difficult, because to answer correctly a person has to mentally override the impulse to read the word. This same effort to override what one reads is what is needed for commitment. A person must use one's mental capacity to stay focused on the task and create the habit for follow-through and commitment. This ability for follow-through and commitment also requires self-regulation and the ability to do things that are not immediately rewarding, or to do things that are more or less uncomfortable or even simply inconvenient. In other words, being committed is not easy. Biologically, commitment requires a healthy mind (or prefrontal cortex) and something you want to commit to.

Organizational commitment comes in three varieties:

1. **Normative.** The desire to conform. A sense of obligation to the company and the extent to which an individual identifies with the specific work tasks and responsibilities that make up the job.

2. **Economic.** The desire to avoid the cost of leaving. A connection based on the cost associated with leaving the current situation for future work and career.

3. **Emotional.** The desire to have an emotional attachment to an organization for whatever reason. A connection to the psychological strength received when working with the organization.

Leaders often wonder just how committed they should be to an organization. In the Academy Award–winning film *The Godfather*, Michael Corleone (the youngest son of Don Vito Corleone and the future head of the Corleone crime family) turns to his brother as the ruthless boss and says, "It's not personal, Sonny. It's strictly business." If what we now know about commitment remains true, then leadership is not "strictly business." It is personal, because leaders must be personally committed to what they are doing to achieve the results they desire. Complete separation of business and personal affairs does not exist because we are more than the body we bring to work each day. The leader's entire person is at play when focusing on commitment.

Being a committed leader to an organization depends in part on:

- Leadership effectiveness and supervision.
- Work environment.
- Adequacy of the technology and resources available.
- Compensation and benefits.
- Teamwork and work process effectiveness.
- Communications and decision making.
- Job content and satisfaction.
- Work/life balance and flexibility.
- Diversity of thinking.
- Ability to perform and advance in learning.
- Culture aligned to personal values.

Substantial research supports the claim that organizations with more committed employees outperform in sales and financial performance. Committed employees stay at their company longer, work harder, and deliver "on-brand" work every day. They do this because they are more satisfied, productive, and active in serving customers. They are more confident and agile in their thinking, and they calculate risks and pursue new opportunities more fully.

THEORY IN PRACTICE ACTIVITY 3.9

EIGHT KEYS OF COMMITMENT

Commitment is described as a desire to make an obligation or pledge, to carry out some action, or to support some policy or person. A committed person has the inner strength to pursue the objective or task and remain focused to work hard without giving up. They consistently give attention to quality work. The ten keys of commitment presented in this Theory In Practice Activity are based on extensive global research with investigated personality traits of committed individuals.

Objective of this exercise: To help you investigate your interest in being a committed leader.

Instructions:

Step 1: Rate your level of response to the eight keys to commitment below. Rather than placing an X in the appropriate box to record your response, shade in all the boxes ending with the box that is your answer. For instance, in the example below, if we wanted to mark our answer as "4," we would shade in the areas 1, 2, 3, and end with 4.

Example:

1 = not often; 2 = sometimes; 3 = often; 4 = very often; 5 = always

The Eight Keys of Commitment	1	2	3	4	5
1. Adapts to other's demands I have an interest in being responsible, productive and effective.	▓	▓	▓	▓	

Assessing Your Level of Commitment

1 = not often 2 = sometimes 3 = often 4 = very often 5 =always

The Eight Keys of Commitment	1	2	3	4	5
1. Adapts to other's demands: I have an interest in being responsible, productive, and effective.					
2. Agreeableness: I am eager to help others. People describe me as being softhearted, good natured, trusting, helpful, forgiving, and empathic.					

3. **Awareness of expectations by others:** I pay attention to meeting the exact expectations or requirements of others.				
4. **Caring and investing:** I have a strong sense of the past and also focus on the long-term perspective.				
5. **Collaboration:** I focus on mutual and reciprocal commitment to goals and objectives by valuing teamwork, consensus, inclusiveness, and investment in others.				
6. **Having a sense of community:** I am concerned and aware of how others would like things done, attending to the group's values and expectations.				
7. **Respectful response:** I am responsible and want to satisfy obligations.				
8. **Service and support:** I enjoy helping and supporting others to meet their particular needs.				

Step 2: Once you have shaded in all the boxes, step back and look at the pattern that emerged from your answers. How would you answer the following questions?

- Are you consistently a committed person?

- Are you only committed in some areas? Why?

- Are there certain environments in which you might be more comfortable being committed?

- Are there certain people toward whom you might be more committed?

- What situations make you more committed than others?

- How does your commitment level affect your ability as a leader?

- After completing this Theory In Practice Activity, what do you plan to do differently from this point forward?

The Committed Question

This discussion supports the competencies of the Champion and our thinking about gaining commitment. A leader with these abilities can easily answer the question, "How can I enhance my commitment and in turn enhance shareholder value?"

12

CHAMPION COMPETENCY #6

Champions confront fear, pain, danger, and uncertainty with strength and perseverance. They are willing to take risks and consider new and untested approaches while exploring the unknown. They are free to respectfully vocalize perspectives without restraint or fear of reprimand or censure. They welcome new ideas and perspectives because of their experimental attitude.

We define "courage" as the resistance to fear and define "courageous actions" as those driven by character. The Champions we have met address the tough double-standard issues and do not bury their heads in the sand and then go numb. To us, no matter how intellectually skilled, emotionally gifted, or economically advantaged a leader is, no one is prepared for all the uncertainty and newness an organization can throw at them. They must act with courage in order to achieve what is best. These leaders know what they want, more than knowing how to get what they want.

The word "courage" came from the Old French word *corage*, meaning "heart and spirit." This would make courage a state of being, where a leader is willing to act from an inner place within his personality and to blaze a trail in support of the principles that benefit the entire organization. Sometimes we wonder if courage is a forgotten virtue of leadership. When we ask most people to think of leadership virtues, they mention honesty, integrity, humor, and authenticity. Courage is rarely mentioned. This forgotten virtue is an admirable feature and a commendable quality of moral excellence, because a leader must be courageous to lead. The courageous leader is required to step up and speak out on questionable situations, in spite of the potential personal costs. This leader must display integrity and assertiveness, so that followers also begin to understand and practice the art of being courageous.

AGILE ILLUSTRATION

While working with Leighton Asia Limited (part of Australia's largest project development and contracting group), we were talking with one of our clients, Mark Moran. At the time, Mark was the project director of the City of Dreams Casino, a US$3 billion megaproject being built in Macau, Special Administrative Region of China. Without question, Mark is an Agile Business Leader, both in his perspective toward leadership and in his actions. Consider his statements on courage:

> As a leader, it's not about making friends. It's about having the courage to set a precedent. Sometimes decisions are made for their own sake rather than thinking through the ramifications and understanding if it makes good business sense. Leaders who are tolerant and don't have the courage to make the right decision aren't really leaders. In my mind, tolerance is bigotry with political correctness. Bigotry is about a person intolerantly devoted to his or her own opinions or beliefs. In practical terms, bigotry is about how you relate to someone who disagrees with you. Despite what individuals want to believe, tolerance does not include appreciation and respect for differences, unless of course one argues that putting up with something is synonymous with appreciating it. I advocate that we have the courage to spend less time voicing what we will and will not tolerate and examine differences as a means of accepting them, rather than hiding behind a concept as an attempt to accept diversity and reconcile with people. Have the courage to stand for something. To me, tolerating a person or action pronounces them as inferior and therefore segregates them. Instead, I suggest to my staff that we celebrate our differences, because tolerance simply allows us to emphasize them. I encourage staff to also have courage to make judgments and have opinions, with the assurance that we all have nothing to hide; we only have points to value. The idea of tolerance legitimizes our prejudices and destroys our real mission of being a democratic culture. Courageous actions are driven by character, and it doesn't involve not taking a stand for something.

Some people mistakenly think courage is relevant only during particularly risky times, such as transitions, product launches, or mergers. The Champion recognizes that exploring new ideas, confronting gossip, transcending rejection, and taking initiative are also courageous leadership moments. Nelson Mandela, the former president of South Africa and the first to be elected in fully representative democratic elections, said, "Courage is not the absence of fear. Instead it is inspiring others to move beyond it." When a leader in the Champion role thinks about being courageous, he knows there is no guarantee for the future, but the past gives him confidence. The Champion knows that "the rearview mirror is usually clearer than the windshield."

We are not for a moment suggesting courage is easy. The risks and pains associated with courage are not to be discredited. Standing alone for a cause and being rejected because of that commitment can hurt. In fact rejection can feel like spilling hot coffee on your arm:

Before you groan and sign and say "I know, I know, let me tell you about the time you-know-who did you-know-what to me," let us clarify. Rejection actually physically hurts. Like dropping something on your toe or getting lemon juice in a paper cut hurts. This is true, according to science, and according to the *New York Times*, which reports on how badly rejection hurts, and how science knows this.

According to a recent study, areas of the brain that indicate physical pain are activated "at moments of intense social loss." In terms of the actual study, forty volunteers (who all felt "intensely rejected" due to a recent breakup) were hooked up to MRI scanners to measure their brain activity while they looked at photos of former boy-friends/girlfriends and thought about exactly how they'd been rejected. (Man, science is mean.) Then they were asked to look at a picture of a friend and think of a good experience with that person.

After all that, they "experienced noxious thermal stimula-tion on their left forearms," which basically means it feels like they spilled hot coffee on themselves. Then they re-ceived "nonnoxious" stimulation, which feels, probably, like a nice warm bath, or at least not as noxious as hot cof-fee. (Source: Disinfo.com)

(Retrieved December 9, 2011 from
http://www.disinfo.com/2011/05/rejection-feels-like-spilling-hot-coffee-on-your-arm/)

The role of Champion is part confidant, part mentor, part rulekeep-er and taskmaster, and part juggler. At the same time, a Champion has the courage to be a steward for the organization, its sharehold-ers, its leaders, and its employees.

We often tell clients, "Bartering your reputation makes it harder to reclaim." A competent leader who is *unwilling* to be courageous and take action is ineffective, inadequate, and useless. That type of reputation will not keep a leader in the leadership role for long. While others are running for cover, the leader with courage is willing to do what he thinks is right and take responsibility for the outcome. Hiding personal courage drains vital energy from the organization the type of vital energy that creates imaginative thinking, wise decision-making, sound dedication, and the building of a common vision. The comedian Louie C.K. is fond of saying, "I only have the courage for a perfect life!"

We suggest that you think of courage as a type of endurance of the soul. Champions face many crucibles in their role, and crucibles have no regard for age, gender, generation, nationality, talent, or charisma. Nelson Mandela, former president of South Africa, said, "The greatest glory in living lies not in never falling, but in rising every time we fall." The willingness to rise every time we fall requires courage.

THEORY IN PRACTICE ACTIVITY 3.10
RIDING HIGH IN THE SADDLE

Objective of this exercise: To provide six steps for increasing courage, with the goal of achieving and accomplishing more and with less difficulty. As actor John Wayne said, "Courage is being scared to death . . . and saddling up anyway."

Instructions:

Step 1: Name It

What worries you most about doing or not doing the action you want to do? In other words, what are you afraid might happen if you proceed with your plan of action?

_____

Remember: Courage is not the absence of fear or despair, but the strength to conquer it. Acknowledge and accept your fears, so that you can move forward to enhancing your ride in the saddle.

Step 2: Visualize It

What does courage look like to you? Name some people who have shown courage, or draw a symbol or picture of what it means to have courage or be courageous.

Remember: The word "courage" derives from the Old French word *corage*, meaning "heart and spirit." This makes courage an innate quality that resides within the core of every human being. Courage exists in you, so saddle up and ride high!

Step 3: Expect It

What if the result of you acting with courage was positive? How would you walk, talk, stand, and act, if you completed the action successfully?

Remember: When you expect a positive result, you walk, speak, and present yourself differently, which influences how others respond to you. In other words, don't slouch in the saddle. Sit up straight and ride tall.

Step 4: Risk It

What would be a good first step in moving forward?

Remember: Take smart risks, not bad ones. When you start off with small acts of courage, your courage grows and eventually you become more comfortable with being courageous and riding in the saddle. Trust yourself to succeed. As British author Malcolm Muggeridge said, "Never forget that only dead fish swim with the stream."

Step 5: Own It

What are you doing or not doing to be a courageous leader?

_____

Remember: Take accountability for your successes and failures. Owning your actions takes courage and shows that you're a true leader.

While it's much easier, giving up is not an option. It takes courage to persist. Being persistent despite discouragement takes great courage.

Step 6: Continue It

What reminders can I use to keep me acting on my beliefs and ideas?

_____

Remember: Riding high in a saddle requires balance, flexibility, coordination, endurance, exertion, strength, and the ability to react. It takes courage to put faith in yourself. The worst decision you can make is to do nothing. Take risks and know that you can succeed. Courage is like a muscle. The more you use it, the stronger your courage becomes.

Champions have a solid sense of what is right and what is wrong, as well as the moral courage to stick to their values even through difficult times. When times are tough and hard decisions need to be made, Champions step forward and make the call. If you ask a Champion, "What do you stand for?" and "What are you going to do?" the Champion will have an answer with substance.

AGILE ILLUSTRATION

We had an opportunity to talk with Navy Rear Admiral Thomas Zelibor, who is the director of global operations for the U.S. Strategic Command. Admiral Zelibor sees his role as a leader as having ultimate responsibility:

> Whatever action you have taken, you have to live with it. In the military, if you screw up, someone may die. Accountability and commitment are ingrained in you; it's part of your makeup and your moral fiber. There is something that goes on in my gray matter when it comes to commitment. I've been in combat a couple of times. I take being committed to my men personally. I weigh the pros and cons and make a decision, and then I take it on. I'm willing to do

the right thing and pay back to my country. It's about self-discipline. Committed people have to know they have an effect on people. We select accountable and committed people in the navy because they can't have a lapse in judgment. Not being there is no excuse. You need to be committed.

The Champion who acts with courage is:

- Clear and acts on what matters most, even when risks are high.

- Acts decisively when deepest values are at stake.

- Remains courageous in the face of strong opposition.

- Acknowledges and learns from mistakes by modifying actions to align with his and the organization's values.

The more Champions see themselves as courageous, even in the tiniest choices, the more self-respect they gain and the more distinctive they become in tough times. They understand that when their integrity is violated, they will not be respected nor will they be trusted. If values are the soul of an organization, then Champi-

ons personify those values and characterize the strength of the organization by acting with courage.

13

CHAMPION COMPETENCY #7

▲ Achieve with Self-Determination ▼

Champions have a passionate purpose. They know what they want, why they want it, and how to communicate their needs to achieve their goals. They operate with a good deal of energy and intensity. ABLs have the discipline to consistently deliver customer value by holding high expectations of themselves and others.

We define the self-determined Champion from two perspectives:

1. **Personal.** Determining one's own course of action without being influenced or pressured. Having free will to act.

2. **Group.** Having freedom and knowledge to self-govern as a group and determine the group's own status.

The self-determined Champion is engaged in activities with a full sense of wanting to do them, choosing to do them, and personally endorsing the actions. Amos Namanga Ngongi, president of the Alliance for a Green Revolution in Africa (AGRA), said during a conference we were helping to facilitate, "I believe in miracles, but if there is one miracle I don't believe in, it is the miracle of succeeding without doing anything." When the self-determined Champion does something, she expresses and acts in accordance with what she truly is. The Champion's choices are not forced upon her. Instead, such a leader chooses to engage in interesting work and activities. The Champion has the capacity to override other deterrents or evaluate reasons for doing things and, instead, makes conscious choices based on her own free will or preference. Behavior for the Champion is intentional, purposeful, and *not* random.

The self-determined Champion excels by:

- **Acting with agility**—having a quick, resourceful, and adaptable character.

- **Being self-directed**—being capable of meeting one's own needs and having confidence in one's personal ability and self-worth.

- **Instigating with wisdom**—comprehending, discerning, and responding with full potential.

- **Being self-aware**—being cognizant and vigilant in observing and drawing inferences from personal experiences.

Most of us rely on others or our business systems to do things for us and enhance the quality of our lives. The distinction of self-determination is about knowing and valuing yourself and not completely relying on others. Champions know they will do well, know what they like and know what they do not do well. They have the wisdom to associate and partner with people to manage different circumstances and succeed.

One of the most common misperceptions about self-determination is that it means doing it all yourself and having absolute control. Some people think that self-determination is equated to independent performance. Self-determination is not about doing everything yourself. Instead it is about making things happen in your life and being able to solve the most complex problems or make complex decisions using the resources you have at hand. Self-determined Champions make things happen by voicing preferences, participating in decisions that impact their actions, and establishing goals to govern aspects of their personal lives and careers.

AGILE ILLUSTRATION

Self-determination for leadership is fundamentally an exercise in *collective* self-determination. To emphasize this point, we had an opportunity to interview a self-determined Champion, Jeff Daniels. Jeff is a retired professional ice hockey player. He was the assistant coach for the Carolina Hurricanes National Hockey League team when they won the Stanley Cup championship trophy in 2006. The Stanley Cup is the oldest professional sports trophy in North America and is achieved by winning the best of seven games in a playoff series. In 2006, the Eastern Conference champions, the Edmonton Oilers, played against the Western Conference champions, the Carolina Hurricanes. The Hurricanes lost games 3, 5, and 6, which meant that Game 7 would be the deciding game for winning the Stanley Cup.

The hockey season starts in September, and by October 2005, the sports experts' predictions were giving no hope to the Carolina Hurricanes for even making the playoffs. The only hope for winning the Cup came from the self-determination of the Hurricanes' team members and the team's coaches.

The path for the Hurricanes to win the Stanley Cup on June 21, 2006, was long and memorable. Some say that the game will go down as one of the most intense and memorable moments in hockey history. In the end, it was all about having the heart and collective self-determination of a champion. Success in winning was due to a massive team effort and the talent and professionalism of everyone involved. The team had one goal in mind—to win the Stanley Cup. Their mantra during the nine-month season was "Whatever it takes."

Jeff Daniels spent time talking with us about leadership and how he helped lead the Hurricanes to the Stanley Cup victory. Beyond the obvious connection of "being agile"—keeping the players physically agile and in top condition to maneuver and position the puck—Jeff also helped keep the team and individual players mentally agile by staying focused, motivated, and connected, and constantly improving their skills.

Jeff was quick to tell us that you can lead by being vocal, but talk is cheap.

> You have to lead by example and be the person the team looks up to when they could be doing something else. I believe leaders must earn respect based on the effort and commitment they personally make to the team. It is the passion for hockey that makes the players come in and do their work. You have to put your ego as a leader aside and

put the team first. You are the one who can use your expertise to help the team perform at its top level. Being a champion is not just about having skill. More importantly, it's
about having character and attitude. You can have all the
skill in the world, but if the person doesn't have a strong,
self-determined character, then you are wasting your time
with skill. We want players and coaches who are not self-
ish. We want them committed to the team.

I would say there are seven key elements that make up a
champion's character:

1. Ability to work with people.

The game of hockey is as much mental as it is physical. If
you want to be a good coach and leader, you have to understand psychology. You have to understand people. When
you have twenty guys on the team with twenty different
personalities, you have to know your team and what will be
the best way to deal with every individual. You have to be
flexible when you lead people. Some people need a kick in
the butt to work toward a common goal; others might need
encouragement. The leader has to know what will be the
best method to get the person motivated. For me, I watch
how people react in different situations. That way, when it
happens to me, I have a better way of handling the person.
Within every group there are different personalities, but as
long as they are working together toward a certain goal, it
will work out. You've got to know your team; you've got
to know and understand your personnel. A good leader
knows how to build a connection with people.

This element leads to increased individual performance.

2. Possess a strong work ethic.

Champions show up every day and practice every day to improve. They come to camp in shape and ready to go, rather than beginning their training when camp starts; they work for both themselves and the team. We spend time getting to know each other and developing a strong connection. Then we bring our families into the group. This is all about getting to know one another and to care for one another. Players respect each other because they have become part of a strong family during the season.

Being a champion is about making sacrifices. When you are a professional athlete and you are in season, you are committed to the team, and that team has a common goal. Professional sport is not all glamorous. You work to provide a good life for your family, but sacrifices have to be made, and you miss out on a lot of things. With a strong work ethic, you put all your time and effort into the season, and often you miss a lot in your personal life, like birthdays, graduations, and free time with the family. But that balances out in the off-season.

Champions are held accountable because they know it's all about the team. They know you are going to war each night, and you need to watch each other's back. That can only happen when you have a strong work ethic and feel accountable to each other. There are a lot of things you can't control, but the one thing you can control is how you work. Make sure you show up. You have to keep working. Having a strong work ethic lets your team know you will never quit.

This element creates commitment.

3. Have confidence.

Suppose you are an NHL player and in the playoffs for a good reason. You have to feel good about yourself and know you are capable. You have to play to your strengths. That's what creates the pride factor. Being confident is important in making a good impression and in making the team believe it can win. When a leader has to stand up and say something hard, you **[QY: the leader? Why would the leader take his own words personally? Please sort out who is saying what to whom here.]** must have the confidence to not take it personally when others disagree with your thinking.. You can't let it get to you. You have to know that the message you give is for the team to do better. The Champion has to stand up and say some hard things and face the music when things aren't going well, and that takes confidence.

This element creates courage.

4. Focus on high expectations.

If things aren't going the way you want, you have to understand your main goal and be flexible on how you are going to get there. It's about not getting too high and excited and not getting too low and discouraged. You must just stay focused on what you want to achieve. It's a long year, and another game is always around the corner. The Champion stays focused and isn't distracted by outside disruptions. I give that message to my team from day one: Stay focused! You may be the champion for one season, but when a new season starts up, you are back at ground zero. Everyone starts the drill again. I let them know that last year is over, and there's nothing we can do about it. Right from day one, I set my expectations for the team and help the players get focused. It doesn't matter whether you won or lost the previous year; each season you begin again with high expectations. You have to ask yourself, "Are you happy to be a champion for one year or to be the best each year?" The biggest thing is that you want to bring the team together, so you have to build a system and give expectations to the team and to individuals.

This element creates results.

5. Self-motivation.

A Champion is personally motivated. Champions say, "I personally want to succeed and be the best at whatever I'm doing. I love the game, and I know I have to make hard sacrifices, and I want to do it." As a coach, I know we all sacrifice our time, our bodies, and our personal lives during the season to become champions.

This element leads to determination.

6. Positive attitude.

As a leader and a Champion, you have to stay positive and upbeat and keep your players positive and upbeat. Sometimes I will go over and whisper to a guy, "Keep your head up." Sometimes I call out a positive message. You have to show the team that you are positive. Being bitter and sad with your head down doesn't help them. When you are positive, you help keep the team relaxed and let them believe things can happen. Being relaxed helps the players be better at what they do. The team members respect you as a leader because they know you are doing whatever it takes to make them succeed. They know that you are there for them and that you will make sure they are prepared to perform.

This element leads to reenergizing self and team.

7. Continually wanting to improve.

A Champion is not about being settled. Champions aren't typically content because they continually want to improve. I can pick out Champions. They are the guys who are there for the right reasons. They are there to work and are there to improve. They are the people who are at the rink before and after games and practices, working on their game. They always want to keep improving. They might watch an extra video because they want to learn, or they might practice some new moves they just learned. They might go to seminars or analyze what they see. Players know the way the game is played; that's not going to change. But how you use your talent within the game can change. Champions aren't satisfied that they have learned it all. You can always learn about a new gadget or technique. Champions are always looking at how they can improve. They don't settle.

This element leads to excellence.

During the last minute of Game 7 in that famous Stanley Cup championship game, time out was called and Jeff drew up a play he thought the Edmonton Oilers would execute and one that the Hurricanes could respond to.

I just reacted; I jumped into the fire and believed in what needed to be done. I reacted in the biggest game of the year and had the confidence and self-determination to do it. I believed in myself and believed in what would happen. When the team went back on the ice, they got the puck after the faceoff, and we were able to score. It wasn't the outcome that made that decision so important. It was the fact that I had the confidence to do it as a leader and coach, and it was a decision that was right for the team.

Collective self-determination is what makes the Champion acquire, achieve, overcome, reach goals, and succeed. Another way to look at self-determination is leaders enabling themselves to become self-governing in order to positively achieve outcomes. Champions have control over themselves, their environment, and the activities that impact their lives. A goal-oriented mind-set helps to initiate and achieve longer-term outcomes.

Any motivational psychologist discussing goal setting will tell you that it is critical to set significant, achievable targets for improvement. Without pushing oneself to achieve progressively better performance in any endeavor, the result is stagnation. At the same time setting unrealistic and unachievable targets is no better. Striving for and then failing to achieve one's goals leads to demotivation.

Without question, leaders who are more self-determined achieve more positive outcomes. Researchers Wehmeyer, Schwartz, and Palmer found that a person who had a greater level of self-determination had greater academic success, better mental health, and enhanced motivation, and was more likely to set and achieve goals.

Skills needed for being a self-determined Champion include the following:

- Choice making

- Decision making

- Problem solving

- Goal setting

- Independence

- Risk taking

- Self-awareness, -evaluation, and -reinforcement

- Self-esteem

- Self-regulation

THEORY IN PRACTICE ACTIVITY 3.11
CAUSE AND EFFECT

Objective of this exercise: To explain how personal perceptions causing actions and events can determine the reason for effective or ineffective performance.

Instructions: Self-determination includes concepts such as free will, independence, self-direction, and individual responsibility. The self-determined leader has an uncanny ability to improvise and adapt to significant changes. They have the ability to accurately attribute the cause of their success to specific conditions. For this Theory in practice follow the next three steps.

Step 1: Give your response to the twenty statements in the table below. For each statement:

Write 4 if you strongly feel this way.

Write 3 if you generally feel this way.

Write 2 if you somewhat feel this way (and somewhat not).

Write 1 if you slightly feel this way.

	I CAUSE RESULTS TO HAPPEN	AMBIGUOUS FACTORS CAUSE RESULTS
The cause of my success is variable	**I choose to exert *effort* to create results.** 1. ___My success or failure depends mostly on the amount of effort I put forth. 2. ___The course of my career largely depends on me. 3. ___Successful completion of assignments is mainly due to my detailed planning and hard work. 4. ___I can largely determine what I will value in the organization. 5. ___My promotion in the organization depends mostly on my ability and effort. **Total score:_____**	**Results are caused by *luck*.** 11. ___From my experience, most things in the organization are beyond one's control. 12. ___My career, to a great extent, is a matter of chance. 13. ___Getting promoted largely depends on me being in the right place at the right time. 14. ___A person's success depends on the breaks or chances he gets. 15. ___The organization you belong to or the job you get is, to a large extent, accidental. **Total score:_____**

	I CAUSE RESULTS TO HAPPEN.	**AMBIGUOUS FACTORS CAUSE RESULTS**
The cause of my success is con-sistent.	**I achieve because of my *ability*.** 6. ___I can largely deter-mine what matters to me in the organization. **[QY: How does this differ from number 4?]** 7. ___My success, to a large extent, depends on my competence and hard work. **[QY: see number 3.]** 8. ___My acceptability to others depends on my behavior with them. 9. ___I can work hard enough to get my sugges-tions accepted in the or-ganization. 10. ___Usually I am responsible for getting or not getting rewards. **Total score:_____**	**Results caused by *difficulty of task*.** 16. ___My effectiveness in this organization is mostly determined by people in senior roles. 17. ___The people who are important in this organiza-tion control things around here. 18. ___To a large extent, my career depends on my supervisors. 19. ___My ideas get accepted if I make them fit with the desires of my su-pervisors. 20. ___My success or failure depends mostly on those who work with me. **Total score:_____**
	Total score _____ for "I cause results to hap-pen" *(statements 1–10)*	**Total score _____ for "Ambiguous factors cause results"** *(statements 11–20).*

Step 2: Total your scores for each of the sections.

Step 3: Interpret your scores from the lists below to determine your level of resilience as an Agile Business Leader. Understanding your level of resilience can help keep you grounded in reality and prevent pessimistic and hostile tendencies.

Total score for "I cause results to happen."

A score of 30–40 implies that you are very confident and believe in your abilities. You are resilient. As a word of caution, sometimes you can be unrealistic and blame yourself for any failure that occurs.

A score of 20–29 implies difficulty in using your full potential. You could be more resilient by making an effort to use your efforts to achieve goals. As a word of caution, you might find that you attribute your success primarily to a contingency plan and nothing else.

A score of 10–19 implies a lack of belief in your own abilities. You may often need the feedback from others to evaluate your strengths. As a word of caution, you may not trust your abilities and not be willing to be accountable for the results. It would be wise to increase your level of resilience by seeking out more challenges and opportunities.

In Summary

Individuals with high scores in this row tend to be high achievers. They work harder and persevere longer in order to get what they want. They approach rather than avoid tasks related to success because they believe success is due to high ability and effort. These leaders gain resilience by making their own decisions, rather than letting others do it for them.

Total score for "Ambiguous factors cause results."

A score of 30–40 implies that you may assume that success is related to causes beyond your control. You are resilient and not overwhelmed by adversity. As a word of caution, there is a tendency with this score to perceive the cause of success to be outside of your control, and you may be reluctant to attempt new tasks. You may also lose motivation to perform well in the workplace.

A score of 20–29 implies a realistic dependence on significant others or fate. You could be more resilient by persevering in finding solutions to difficult issues. As a word of caution, you might find that you attribute your success to other factors beyond your control, which can negatively impact your resilience.

A score of 10–19 implies that it may be difficult for you to handle unforeseen situations. Success may not seem rewarding because you do not feel responsible for the results. This could affect your pride and confidence in undertaking a task. You may become frustrated when unforeseen contingencies or situations come your way. It would be wise to increase your level of resilience by being more assertive, decisive, and self-motivated.

In Summary

Individuals with high scores in this row have developed learned resourcefulness. They are resilient and are not overwhelmed by adversity. They approach external issues (forces in economy, competitors, weather, technology) as being beyond their control. Resilience comes from rebounding quickly following defeats and cop-ing well with frequent frustrations, rejection, and stress.

Recognize the basic fact that you always have a choice. Making no choice is actually a choice in and of itself, and it's your choice when you allow other people or events to make your decisions for you.

Being self-determined is not only about acquiring the knowledge and skills to achieve; it is also about having the attitudes, beliefs, and perceptions that Champions bring into the role of a leader. These attitudes enhance the Champion's perceptions of control, self-reliance, individualism, and choice, all of which enable him or her to acquire those skills and knowledge and lead to greater things. Champions engage in activities that enable the exertion of greater control over their lives.

14

CONCLUSION

Being a Champion is a leadership component that is all but forgotten by modern standards. Corporations tend to value leaders who are rational, strategic thinkers and system developers. They value the people who run the organization. We suggest that the Champion creates the organization. The Champion's role is about the character of the leader. It is about the essence of who the leader is as a person. Being a Champion goes beyond actions. If values are the soul of an organization, then the Champion personifies those values and characterizes the strength of the organization through personal character.

We propose that Champions have four specific character traits that become valuable assets to any organization. These characteristics are critical to the future success of any organization. The four traits of the Champion are:

1. Resourcefulness
2. Responsiveness
3. Resilience
4. Commitment

Many people pay lip service to the idea that leading an organization requires strength of character. We claim that character is central to being a leader. The character of a Champion includes the emotional fortitude to be honest with oneself, with others in business, and with the realities of the organization. Champions are open to whatever information they need, whether they like to hear it or not. They have the courage to accept points of view that are the opposite of theirs and to deal with conflict. Champions have the strength to accept and to deal with their own weaknesses and the courage to be firm with people who are not performing. They can handle ambiguity, which is inherent in any fast-moving, complex organization. The multitude of characteristics included in this book encapsulate what makes up the character of the Champion. In the words of Warren Buffett, investor, philanthropist, and one of the richest men in the world, "The road that leads to great success is usually paved with a ton of mistakes, so get over it and on with it. If you don't like leading, you can always follow." The Champion likes to lead and has the character to lead in an exemplary manner.

IDEAS IN ACTION

When working with several leaders in developing what is now the role of Champion, Jeremy Kidner and Barry developed a program called "The Race Is On!" (TRIO) which uses Cartaphors to open up thinking and create action plans for personal and organizational change.

The Race Is On! is based on Formula One (F1) racing. It helps businesses at the individual, team, and organizational levels develop a commitment to

- Improve performance and efficiency.
- Create ideas and innovations.
- Create or maintain a competitive future.

The program uses F1 Cartaphors to provoke honesty, openness, and creative thinking in assessing the current state of a business and in developing a strategy for change. The following is an extract from that program.

INTRODUCTION

F1 teams compete to win. Winning teams get more sponsorships and therefore make more money. But, as cars get faster and safer, races become less exciting, and people stop watching. But getting the teams to agree to changes leads to endless arguments. Competitive behavior does not mean that the needs of the customer, the spectator, are met.

By using an F1 analogy, teams discover when they need to coordinate their activities (e.g., process improvements), when they need to collaborate (e.g., to come up with new products or to create new markets), and when they need to change what they do (e.g., design their own processes, create their own software, move up the value chain, launch a new brand, design and build cars for their markets).

Whether it's cars, consumer products, luxury products, or financial services, companies can compete globally. Successful companies don't rely on protection, geography, or history to do so.

"If everything's under control, you're not going fast enough!"
-Michael Schumacher, British F1 driver

SETTING THE SCENE

F1 teams typically employ between 600 and 900 people, mostly at the "factory," a term used to describe the head office, workshops and development centers. Of the 900 people, about 150 to 180 work trackside, meaning that they are involved in the racing at the various circuits.

In order to be successful, teams must have outstanding drivers and cars; the teams need to coordinate their activities very closely when they race, particularly during the pit stops when the cars are refueled and fitted with new tires. Fractions of a second lost on a pit stop can make the difference between winning and losing a race. Also, when racing, teams need to have a superior race strategy—when to pit, how much fuel to take on, whether to apply more or less down-force on the wings, and so on.

DEVELOPMENT

Building a successful team takes years. The technology in the cars is space age—for example, the engines rev up to 19,000 rpm, about seven or eight times faster than road cars commuting to the office.

Teams employ highly skilled technicians and designers, many of whom are kept nameless so that they aren't poached by other teams.

The interesting aspect of F1 is that as the cars get faster, competition actually is decreasing, so races become less interesting and TV audiences—the lifeblood of the sport—may drift away. Teams have to learn to compete differently, and leaders must champion the cause.

ORGANIZATIONAL TEAMS

Organizations are not unlike F1 teams. They have operations on the ground—the equivalent of cars, drivers, and mechanics at the racetrack. Their success depends on these people.

They have factories, varying from conventional factories actually making things to offices in which people work and provide services. Like the skilled people supporting the development of a racing team, these people are the future of the organization in the sense that they support the crew and develop the way to the future.

Organizations also have team bosses, typically a CEO or a managing director who works with senior teams to manage the whole organization. Organizations have sponsors and customers (equivalent of spectators).

On the day of the race, racing cars and their teams need to get it all right—the right choice of tires, the right race strategy, and effective execution. Remember that the race is won as much in the pits as it is on the racetrack, where seconds count. And it's not just one race that wins the championship; it's the whole season.

In the race for customers, competitive products generate profits, either by reducing cost or adding value or a combination of both. These products are driven by people such as sales and service crews or teams. Think of the moments of truth that affect your position in the race for customers every day of the week. Increasingly, companies like Ryanair (is an Irish low-cost airline) Dell, and others have changed customers' expectations in terms of value.

Winning teams are not created overnight. Successful cars are the result of many hours of development back at the factory, where designers and mechanics work on this year's and next year's cars.

It's the same for any organization—commercial or government. You have to think about next year's products or services, which means you have to know which race you want to compete in and how you're going to win customers. But design is one thing; performance is another.

Research has established why some teams outperform others, why some teams become great, and why some—indeed many—teams fail. Much of this comes down to human behavior and the leader's ability to shape behavior.

"Where would your organization be if Ferrari managed the view from the boss's office?" Examine this question in the context of the following three teams:

1. Operations—pit crews and racing drivers—people at the sharp end.

2. Management and support—the team at the factory and the company's suppliers.

3. Senior management—people who run the team.

IMPROVING HOW YOU WIN RACES

As *F1 Racing for Dummies* states, "Pit stops have become one of the most tense and exciting features of a Grand Prix, and races are frequently won and lost in this high-pressure environment."(*F1 Racing For Dummies – p.139*)

In a sport in which speed is all important, it is ironic that races are won and lost when the car is stationary. Certainly, the disorganized chaos of stops during the sport's early days, which saw drivers sneak out of their cars for a brief spell, are a distant memory. And ever since the law on refueling came into effect in 2010, stop times have become even quicker, plummeting from the refueling era's average of around ten seconds to well under five. At the Malaysian Grand Prix in 2010, McLaren posted one of the fastest stops of the season, when it serviced Lewis Hamilton's car in a breathtakingly quick 3.4 seconds.

It's understandable, then, that pit stops are one of Formula One racing's most mesmerizing—and edgy—spectacles. One slip could cost a driver dearly, but conversely, if all goes to plan, it's an invaluable opportunity to gain an advantage over your rivals. Like most things in Formula One racing, the stakes are very high, and from beginning to end, speed and efficiency are crucial.

(Retrieved October 28, 2011 from
http://www.formula1.com/news/features/2011/3/11819.html)

Coordination is very important to the Formula One racing team during a pit stop. Think about the following:

- What happens if the driver doesn't come in when the team is expecting him?

- What would be the effect if the driver left before they had finished putting on all the wheels?

- How dangerous would it be if the driver left while they were still filling the car with fuel?

- What happens if the pit crew doesn't listen to the driver about how the car is performing?

If Ferrari saw your view from the pits, what processes that you are involved in would they do differently?

You know what happens better than anyone in the company. After all, you are required to complete pit stops every day of the week. Take some time and think about the processes you use every day of the week (your pit-stop equivalents). How might they be different if a team from Ferrari were asked to undertake them? How can your team be coordinated better?

Hint: Think about this question at two levels. For example, if a wheel man was asked, he might say that the pit stops could be improved by changing part of the equipment as he had found that by doing this or that he was able to do his job better. But he may also observe that when the team members were loading equipment on and off the transporter, if they changed the order in which equipment was loaded, they might be able to shorten the process. In other words, think about things that affect you, and things you see at a team level that could improve the product or service you are offering in some way to reduce cost, improve service or quality, and so on.

ABOUT YOUR PEOPLE

An F1 team depends almost entirely on its talent. There are two dimensions to hiring people: their suitability (for example, a design specialist may not make a good wheel man in the pit lane) and their eligibility (the wheelman may not have the qualifications necessary for the designer's job). In addition, the teams spend huge amounts of time and money working with teams and cars to get them working well together, just as companies spend time recruiting, training, and developing teamwork.

Consider these questions:

1. Do you think Ferrari would accept your company's approach to recruitment, training, and teamwork? Why?

2. What has stopped you from changing this so far?

3. What would you need to see, hear, or feel to recognize when it was time to do something different?

4. What criteria would you use to decide what needs to change?

5. What should stay the same?

6. What's the difference?

7. How will you know whether you have chosen the right elements for each of these?

PERSONAL ACTION PLAN

Self-assessment and adaptability are extremely important as an Agile Business Leader. We suggest you devise a personal plan to accomplish changes you want to implement for yourself or for your organization. Ask the question, "What actions or changes in my behavior do I need to accomplish and by when?" Then construct an action plan that will help you achieve your goal. Write it down and monitor it, or use your community of practice to help you become even more accountable for your actions.

What actions or changes in my behavior do I need to accomplish? How soon?

Action Plan

	Action Item	Resources Required	Date of Completion
1			
2			
3			
4			

About the Authors

Barry Brewster and Eileen Dowse

EILEEN DOWSE, Ph.D., is a recognized organizational psychologist, specializing in organizational health and effectiveness through training, consulting, cultural assessments, and performance management. She works with individuals, teams, and large-scale systems to facilitate strategic change throughout North America, Europe, Africa and Asia. She fosters productive relationships for organizations and strengthens employee commitment to ensure greater levels of teamwork. She is among the international leaders in facilitation. She is co-founder and chair for the International Institute for Facilitation and a certified master facilitator. Eileen uses common sense wisdom and innovative ideas to offer exceptional professionalism and customized services.

BARRY BREWSTER is a principal with Evans and Peck, a member of the WorleyParson Group, specializing in facilitating change in a variety of business environments. With more than twenty-five years of experience in Asia Pacific, Europe, and North America, he works on optimizing business performance through positive change in strategy, systems, processes, and people. Clients seek out Barry because he successfully helps them leverage the knowledge and wisdom within their organization to produce sustainable results. Barry is a board member of the International Institute for Facilitation and a certified master facilitator. Barry's unique ability to facilitate learning, energize people toward innovation, and bring about change is what makes him an AGILE leader in the industry.

For more information on The Agile Business Leader series of books please contact us www.agilebusinessleader.com

Browse Publishing

Hong Kong

www.ingramcontent.com/pod-product-compliance
Lightning Source LLC
Chambersburg PA
CBHW071632200326
41519CB00012BA/2267